Essential Musical Intelligence

For Barbara,
+ Wally

EMI is the ticket –
the bliss!

Louise Montello

Essential Musical Intelligence

Using Music as Your Path to Healing, Creativity, and Radiant Wholeness

Louise Montello
NCPsyA, CMT

Quest Books
Theosophical Publishing House
Wheaton, Illinois ♦ Chennai (Madras), India

The Theosophical Society wishes to acknowledge the generous support of the Kern Foundation in the publication of this book.

First Quest Edition 2002

The Theosophical Publishing House
P. O. Box 270
Wheaton, Illinois 60189-0270

Library of Congress Cataloging-in-Publication Data

Montello, Louise.
Essential musical intelligence: using music as your path to healing, creativity, and radiant wholeness / Louise Montello.
p. cm.
Includes discography and bibliographical references.
ISBN 0-8356-0814-X
1. Music therapy. 2. Music—Psychological aspects. I. Title.

ML3920 .M67 2002
615.8'5154—dc21 2001048896

Cover image, cover design, and interior design by Dan Doolin

5 4 3 2 1 * 02 03 04 05 06

Printed in the United States of America

Table of Contents

In loving memory of
Jean Scully

Acknowledgments

Countless people have contributed to the conception, gestation, and birthing of this book. To all I send my deepest gratitude and blessings. In particular, I thank my passionate agent, Andrea Pedolsky, who planted within me the seed to write and helped me cultivate and harvest the EMI crop.

With many thanks to the folks at Quest Books: my publisher, Sharron Dorr; publicist Renee Smith; designer Dan Doolin; and my soulful editor, Jane Lawrence.

With special thanks to quintessential musician Rachel Z, who taught me so much about EMI. My deepest gratitude goes out to my friend and mentor, Ted Coons, for his constant love and support. I thank my wonderful "family" at the Himalayan Institute for nurturing my soul; and Sondra Farganis and Gina Walker at New School University for their inspiration and encouragement.

I am also grateful to the incredible teachers who deeply inspired me on the path of music healing: John Beaulieu, John Diamond, Pir Vilayat Khan, Saraswati O'Neill, David Hykes, Susan Osborne, and Barbara Hesser; and to my spiritual guides who assisted me every step of the way in writing this book.

With much love and thanks to Jay Kantor for awakening the researcher within; to John Bell for making the research possible; to Bonnie Hirschhorn for her friendship and nourishing country retreat; and to my bandmates, Peter Matthews, Jeff Fountain, and

Roger Mannin, who helped me to keep my music alive while I was writing this book.

I also thank my family for the gifts of music, laughter, and honest expression that have allowed me the freedom to dance to the beat of my own drummer.

I would especially like to thank the many remarkable students and clients who have graced my life over the years. Without you, this book would not be possible. Lastly, I thank my Essential Musical Intelligence for the constant source of beauty and light that has helped me in understanding and transforming unspeakable darkness.

Foreword

The grace of Essential Musical Intelligence, the highest form of creative power there is, gives not just musicians but all people the chance to heal and transform their lives.

Dr. Louise Montello has created a simple direct approach for reaching into the deepest subconscious mind to free ourselves of pain and suffering caused by abuse, terrorism, neglect, abandonment, and addiction. Her special techniques help us use music to tune in to both the positive and negative shadow aspects of ourselves and to transform our unwieldy and sometimes destructive characteristics. By turning the "poison" in our lives into medicine through our engagement with music, we are able to use this transformed energy as a positive force in healing ourselves and the planet.

Because it directly taps the healing essence of the soul, Essential Musical Intelligence allows us to experience immediate balance. Dr. Montello's practical exercises are designed to show us how to let the joy of music create harmony, safety, peace, and abundance in our lives whenever we need it, each and every day.

The gift of true creativity is no longer a secret to be held by just a few "chosen" musicians. Now everyone can find the secret of connecting to the light of the soul through music. Dr. Montello's discovery of Essential Musical Intelligence is a gift of healing for us all.

—Rachel Z

Pianist, composer, and Sony/RED recording artist

December 2001

A Note to the Reader

Because many of the ideas and concepts presented throughout this book draw from both ancient mystical and contemporary cutting-edge treatises, some of the language may be unfamiliar to you. For help, please see the glossary at the back of the book. There are also appendices listing various resources for assistance in finding things like suitable music and musical instruments, and an alphabetical list of the exercises with page numbers.

In addition, you will find narratives throughout the text featuring clients whose personal journeys illuminate the principles of EMI. Names and personal details have been fictionalized to protect their privacy, but the stories are all true.

For easier reading, please note that I often use "musical intelligence" and "EMI" interchangeably with Essential Musical Intelligence.

Introduction

See deep enough and you see musically,
the heart of nature being everywhere music,
if you can only reach it.
—Thomas Carlyle

The fourteenth-century Sufi poet, Hafiz, once told a story about the sacred origin of music. "In the beginning," Hafiz explained, "God made a clay statue as an image of the Divine and asked the human soul to enter it. The soul refused, regarding this forced incarnation as a kind of imprisonment. The soul was accustomed to fly freely about the celestial realms, unfettered and unbound. So God requested the angels to play their music. The angelic song brought the soul such ecstasy that it willingly entered the body of clay, believing that it would hear the music better in physical form. But," Hafiz continued, "angelic music was more than God's lure. Many say that on hearing the music, the soul entered into the body, but in reality the soul itself was music."[1]

Hafiz' story illuminates the power and mystery of Essential Musical Intelligence, your innate ability to use music and sound to facilitate deeper levels of self-awareness and transformation, leading to mind-body-spirit integration and radiant wholeness. Music not only awakens the life of the soul within you, it actually is the vibrational essence of your soul and of all life. Thus, when you are deeply engaged in playing or listening to music, you naturally detach from the limitations of your rational, linguistic mind and enter into a more creative, symbolic, expanded state of awareness where you become one with the vibration of your soul—the unlimited, all-knowing, infinite core of your being.

In many spiritual and secular traditions, music is revered as the most direct way to make contact with our deeper selves. Think back to some of your own experiences with singing, playing, and listening to music. Do you notice any changes in your body or mind as these memories arise? Some of my most poignant memories include listening to gospel music, chanting the name of God in the Hindu and Sufi traditions, and surrendering to the passion of the moment during improvisational jam sessions. Each of these musical happenings literally sent shivers down my spine and filled me with awe and inexplicable joy. Just imagining them now creates a similar sensation in me, although with much less intensity. During these musical experiences, our souls are touched and awakened. We feel truly whole, quite naturally connecting with a deeper, almost transpersonal reality.

Essential Musical Intelligence is present in all people at birth. Because EMI is associated with the life of the soul, it was most likely present in your reality before birth and will be with you as your soul's essence after death. EMI can be observed in the way an infant spontaneously uses sound and melody to soothe herself when she experiences discomfort or rejoices with a gleeful outburst from the bliss of being fully alive. EMI is activated and used by the toddler as he asserts his own emerging identity separate from Mommy, in the form of little improvised songs that he proudly repeats endlessly throughout the day. It is the driving force behind the phenomenal talent of the musical prodigy and those with savant syndrome. It is also an important catalyst for emotional development in teenagers and young adults.

Somewhere along the line, however, many of us lose our connection with EMI. Each time our belief in our own creative abilities is undermined in some way, especially during our childhood years, we lose a little bit of spirit, which is the wind beneath the wings of musical intelligence. People whose lives are all work and no play are cut off from EMI because they have not allowed themselves the time to just be, to look within and explore the imaginal and archetypal realms outside ordinary consciousness. Even some professional musicians, forced at an early age to give up the joy and freedom of simply playing music in order to perform it, maintain an ambivalent relationship with music.

This book is about how we can all reclaim that connection. As you begin to embrace Essential Musical Intelligence, you will naturally become more responsible in exercising your free will to literally create your own reality. Through connecting with EMI, you will learn to discriminate between the things you have manifested that are in alignment with your soul's path and those that limit your personal growth and freedom of expression. When you have reached this state of self-realization, there is truly no one else to blame for your shortcomings or suffering. This may be a rather rude awakening: we are indeed creatures of habit and, at times, find it difficult to detach from familiar patterns of thinking and feeling, even if they are keeping us stuck in less-than-desirable mental and physical states. But, as you know, resistance to change is a natural human tendency. With time, patience, and practice, EMI will prevail.

Chapter One

Your Essential Musical Intelligence

Essential Musical Intelligence is your natural ability to use music and sound as self-reflecting, transformational tools to facilitate total health and well-being.

Imagine starting your day by finding a tranquil spot in nature where you can sit quietly for a spell and listen with an open heart to the subtly emerging sounds of the pulsating life within and around you that gently reveal to you the secrets of your soul . . .

or

Imagine being alone on a cold winter's night wrapped in a warm blanket and listening to Brahms's *Requiem* with candles burning brightly, asking in your heart for assistance in mourning the loss of a loved one of whom you have not been able to let go . . .

or

Imagine using intentional sound making (toning) to give voice to that persistent pain under your left shoulder blade. Feel the chronic tension melting in the creative heat of your expressive self as you let go and allow the music take you where you need to go . . .

All these scenarios are examples of how you can activate your Essential Musical Intelligence in daily life. They each reflect a certain level of comfort and intimacy that you can develop with the wise, compassionate, and deeply creative capacity of your Higher Self (or soul) through your engagement with music. It is my premise that we become overwhelmed by pain, suffering, and ignorance when we are cut off from our innate divinity, and that deep and lasting healing ensues when we reestablish a conscious relationship with this aspect of ourselves.

Although Essential Musical Intelligence is ubiquitous and instinctual, it will, however, require some effort on your part to *consciously* integrate its potential for healing into your daily life. There are two complementary phases involved in using EMI to facilitate self-healing and transformation.

The first phase, which I call the *witnessing stance,* involves the practice of self-observation and inner listening. Witnessing is the process of turning your focus inward and becoming the observer of the permutations of your mind, body, and emotions, as opposed to living your life on automatic pilot, without much conscious awareness. Witnessing can be honed through the formal practice of meditation, in which you sit quietly for a period of time and watch the flow of mind stuff with a sense of detachment; or it can be practiced informally at selected intervals throughout the day as a way of consciously tuning out the noise of external reality and allowing yourself to gradually tune into the deeper music of your inner self. The process of tuning into your inner music—the emotional and archetypal landscape that colors both waking and dreaming states—is associated with inner listening. In order to achieve full engagement with the witnessing stance of EMI, it is important to cultivate the ability to listen with the ear of the heart—your innate intuitive capacity that allows you to both hear your inner music and at the same time realize its true meaning. For instance, if you find while engaged in the witnessing stance that you are unable to maintain your equanimity and you succumb to mind-body states that are less than desirable (e.g. pain, confusion, despair, psychological numbing), you can call upon your intuitive listening capacity to provide a deeper level of understanding of what is going on inside you.

As you become more skilled at turning inward and engaging the witnessing stance, you will soon become aware of those thoughts, feelings, bodily sensations, and behaviors that foster health and creativity as well as those that detract from your sense of well-being. The witnessing phase of essential musical intelligence involves your willingness to take regular time-outs from the activities of your day and tune into how you are feeling. This can be done upon rising to observe if and how certain somatic states, feelings, and attitudes might influence your daily activities; in the evening before retiring as a way of reviewing the dynamics of your day; or any time during the day when you feel the need for centering and mind-body coherence.

Once your internal feeling states are illuminated and clarified during the witnessing phase, you may then allow yourself to move gently into the deeper, more musical essence of your being, where you can intuitively sense what you need to become more balanced and whole. As you enter this second *transformational phase* of using EMI, you may either consciously choose to engage in specific musical activities that help to create balance and harmony within, or you can allow spontaneous music or sound to emerge from a deeper source (improvisation) as an agent of change in harmonizing and transforming the specific physical, mental, and emotional energies at the root of your problem.

For example, if you have been working hard all day on a research paper and start to feel a suspicious tickle in your throat, you have several choices: you can ignore the tickle and keep pushing yourself to finish the paper; you can suck on a couple of cough drops and continue working; or you can pause, connect with your Essential Musical Intelligence, and be receptive to the message that your body is trying to communicate to you. In the intuitive space of your musical intelligence, you might discover that you are truly tired and require a play break. After some gentle stretching, you put on big-band music and swing yourself around for a few minutes, letting that "fascinating rhythm" take you where you need to go. When you feel pleasantly fatigued, you turn off the music and notice that the tickle is gone. What happened? Most probably, the combination of music and dance had a salutary effect on your immune system, possibly precluding an infection. You feel energized and ready to return to work.

Essential Musical Intelligence can also be engaged to root out and transform painful emotional states. For example, many of us are hampered by performance anxiety, which can affect anything from presenting a report to a roomful of colleagues or meeting with a potential new employer to having dinner with our in-laws! You may try numerous tactics to push the anxiety away, like holding your breath, imagining you are somewhere else, or seeing the audience as a bunch of cantaloupes. When these strategies fail, you may try even stronger remedies like alcohol, tranquilizers, or beta-blockers. But the root cause of the anxiety never goes away. By activating your musical intelligence, you can become aware of the emotional dynamics underlying the anxiety and playfully externalize this energy through some kind of musical improvisation, such as drumming. Once the emotional energy is externalized, understood, and accepted (instead of being feared and/or repressed), then it can be used creatively toward achieving your performance-related goals.

Developing a witness stance is a prerequisite to using EMI for health and healing. There are many exercises that can help to strengthen your capacity to observe the modifications of the mind-body. My favorite one involves breath awareness.

Breath Awareness

Take a few minutes now to observe your breathing. In a comfortable seated position, be aware of the air as it enters your nostrils and again as it leaves your nostrils. Continue to follow the movement of your breath. You might notice some jerks or pauses as you breathe, or even a faint breathing sound. Do not try to change anything—just watch. You may even become impatient and resist this self-reflective activity. That is all right. On your next exhalation, allow the breath to release these impatient feelings, and as you inhale, bring your awareness back to your breath. If any thoughts arise, simply let them go for now and bring your focus back to your breath. Soon you will notice that your consciousness begins to shift. You feel more present and rooted in your body, calmer and more relaxed. You are moving into a state of being versus doing. You have become a witness to your internal states. You will now be able to consciously connect with your Essential Musical Intelligence.

Once you are centered in this witnessing/listening stance, you can continue to engage EMI to address specific health issues, emotional problems, or relationship difficulties from the perspective of your infinitely wise and creative higher self.

Liz was recovering from a debilitating eating disorder. She had been using her Essential Musical Intelligence as a way to change her focus when food cravings emerged and threatened to propel her into a binge. She described to me the power and sacredness of connecting with EMI at a moment of escalating temptation:

> I was on my way to the supermarket to buy food for a binge. I felt dazed and confused but completely controlled by my urge to binge. As I walked, I began to hear the words of the song that we had worked on in therapy: "I know that I can make it . . ." My mind went back to my craving. Then I heard the second line of the song: "I know that I can stand . . ." I heard my Essential Musical Intelligence. For a while there was a battle going on inside, but then EMI won out. I literally began to sing the rest of the song out loud as I walked toward the store, "No matter what may come my way, my life is in Your hands." I kept repeating the verses, and when I arrived at the store, I bought just enough food to prepare a normal healthy meal for myself, nothing extra. I felt blessed and healed and so grateful for the presence of EMI in my life.

Liz had found a gospel tune (Kirk Franklin's "My Life is in Your Hands")[1] that activated her EMI and allowed her to stay connected to spirit even in her darkest moments. When she first brought the song to her therapy session and began to sing while I accompanied her on the piano, she cried uncontrollably for several minutes. When I asked what she was experiencing, she told me that for the first time in her life, she felt she was not alone. As she listened to her own voice connecting with the words of the song, Liz suddenly felt a loving presence radiating throughout her being. In that moment she realized that she had been gorging herself to fill up the emptiness inside, using food to keep her company. Now she knew that she possessed something that could radiate warmth, caring, and love whenever she took the time to listen within—her Essential Musical Intelligence.

One way of deepening your connection with your Essential Musical Intelligence is to keep track of the choices you make on a daily basis in creating your unique musical and emotional environment. How are you using music right now to maintain a sense of emotional and physical balance, to help you to understand yourself better, and to give voice to your creative vision? You can document your relationship with music and sound by keeping a Music and Sound Awareness Journal, where you make daily entries that reflect your expanding capacity to listen with the ear of your heart (intuition) and use music and sound to create and transform your inner and outer realities.

Music and Sound Awareness Journal

Some ideas for journaling might include how and why hearing J. S. Bach's "Air on the G String" at the Pottery Barn changed your mood while you were shopping at the mall; whether Barber's "Adagio for Strings," part of the soundtrack for the movie *Platoon,* affected your mood while you watched the film; what those annoying song fragments that keep running through your mind are really trying to tell you. You can also tune into specific rhythms and sounds that vibrate in the space about you (dishwasher, sirens, a babbling brook) and observe how they affect your equilibrium.

Systematically observe how the other elements of music—tempo, melody, harmony (or lack of it), dynamics, and timbre—influence your body, mind, and spirit as you listen. You might want to actually audiotape your journal so that you can include significant fragments of music that you listen to or recordings of your own music—improvisations, songs, sound making, and other musical creations. You can review the journal tapes later to explore the permutations of your musical work-in-progress and to reconnect with the vibration of your soul during occasional dry spells. It is important to listen to and make music on a daily basis. The more in touch you are with your evolving musical and spiritual life, the greater access you will have to your Essential Musical Intelligence.

A more immediate way to reconnect with your musical intelligence is through conjuring your earliest memory of music. When we are children, listening to music usually evokes a mood of awe, wonder, joy, celebration, and love that we openly share with our parents and loved ones. Thus, for most of us, this earliest memory reflects an aura of safety, security, and trust in the inherent goodness of the world around us. It is often our first conscious experience of the vibration of the deeper self.

After many years of practicing music therapy with people from all walks of life, it often seems to me that this musical memory is like a keynote of the soul's mission or desire in this lifetime. It is uncanny how the emotional quality of the music almost always mirrors the temperament of the individual as he or she moves through life.

For example, Samantha, a bubbly psychiatrist with a passion for dance, literally began to sway in her chair as she connected with her first musical memory of listening to Saint-Saens' *Carnival of the Animals* when she was two years old. She remembered creating special dances for each of the animals while her parents looked on in admiration. Throughout her life, this client had spontaneously used music and dance as a way of playfully connecting with the "beloved child" within.

Another client's earliest musical memory occurred when he was three years old. Adam recalled sitting in a diner with his depressed mother on a dreary Sunday afternoon, listening to Sandra Dee sing "I'm Sorry" on the jukebox. He told me that this memory was strangely comforting and made him feel safe. A songwriter, Adam had a melancholic temperament and suffered from incessant guilt related to his growing success in music. It is interesting to note from the presenting core memory how the life of the soul of this young man was somewhat veiled due to the emotional climate of his early life. The memory helped explain why a more healthy inclination to feel good about his success was overridden by feelings of depression and guilt associated with his early relationship with his mother. The following story illustrates how recovering our earliest memories of music can help restore our relationship with Essential Musical Intelligence.

Anna was at a standstill in therapy over painful issues related to parental abandonment and neglect. She was unable to activate her musical intelligence. I led her through a guided meditation to retrieve her earliest memory of music. The memory came quickly:

> I was very young, riding on the bus with my mother. I was singing "Thumbelina" (from the fairy tale by Hans Christian Andersen) and rocking back and forth on the seat. I must have been in preschool at the time. I remember the bus going by a

park. We were sitting up front behind the driver's seat. It was summer.

I asked Anna to describe the feeling tone of her memory. "It felt good," she replied. "I kept repeating it over and over again. People probably got sick of it."

When she returned from her meditative state, I asked Anna if she could recall any of the words to the song. Incredibly, she remembered all of them, though she hadn't heard them in more than forty years:

Thumbelina, Thumbelina, tiny little thing,
Thumbelina dance, Thumbelina sing.
O Thumbelina, what's the difference if you're very small?
When your heart is full of love, you're nine feet tall.

In processing the memory, Anna realized that even at a tender age, she knew she was different from her parents. She told me that they would sing, but there was no delight in their singing. They weren't able to share in the joy and wonder of singing that Anna experienced. She remembered her mother in particular as distant and numb. Anna eventually internalized that numbness, and as she grew older, forgot about her great love of singing—the natural channel for her Essential Musical Intelligence.

Was little Anna really singing to her mother on that bus, trying to wake her up, to teach her how to love? Did she know somewhere inside that her mother's heart needed to be opened? Why was she so insistent? Why didn't her mother hear her? All these questions ran through my mind as I tried to imagine Anna's early home situation. The answers would come at a later point in Anna's therapy. What was truly important here was the transformational moment when Anna reconnected with the felt experience of her Essential Musical Intelligence that was so alive during childhood. By reconnecting with her earliest memory of music, Anna remembered the love that was an essential part of her nature. It had been buried under layers of numbness for years, keeping her once-boundless joy and passion imprisoned. In reconnecting with EMI, Anna was able to use music, particularly singing, to gradually thaw her numbness into a new zest for life and an ongoing relationship with creative change.

Your Earliest Musical Memory

You can recover your earliest memory of music quite simply. Take a few moments to relax by practicing the witnessing exercise described earlier. Once your thoughts are stilled and your body is calm, allow yourself to travel back in time—as far back as you can possibly remember—and connect with your earliest memory of being with music. It should come quite easily. (If it is difficult for you to retrieve early childhood memories, you might try looking at some childhood photographs.) Pick the very first memory that comes along. Allow this memory to increase in vividness by focusing on the colors, sounds, smells, feelings, and bodily sensations that you experienced then. Write down your impressions in your Music and Sound Awareness Journal.

Did you notice any correlation between that earliest memory and your relationship with music today? What about your temperament, personal mission, the quality of your emotional life? Take a few moments now to contemplate the remarkable self-reflecting quality of music. In your relationship with music, you can discover the origins of your current emotional makeup. As you learn to activate the transformational power of EMI, you can, over time, literally recreate your internal world so that it reflects only the thoughts, feelings, and beliefs that are in alignment with your higher self.

As you begin the process of reconnecting with EMI, it is so important to allow yourself down time on a regular basis so you can let go of the pressing demands of outer reality and surrender to your soul's desire for peace and solitude. It is in these moments of stillness that EMI comes alive. It's really an age-old process.

For example, the Sanskrit language (which is closest to the language of music) was transmitted to the ancient Indian sages while they were engaged in deep states of contemplation and meditation. In ancient Greece, people with physical and emotional ills traveled to the healing temples of Aesclepius where they were lulled into altered states by soothing music that allowed them access to the healer within. In these altered states they received dreams and visions that helped them to symbolically transform the root causes of their pain and suffering, leading to miraculous cures. As you can see, EMI is not activated through the conscious mind but through the realm of imagination, the domain of the soul. In this dimension there is no concept of time. Everything is happening in the eternal now. In this realm there are infinite possibilities to create and transform your reality. The more comfortable you are living and playing in this imaginal world, the more your musical intelligence will manifest its healing presence in your life.

The Heart of EMI

Essential Musical Intelligence is always present in our lives. Its power is most available to us when our hearts are open and we are in a receptive, intuitive, playful, or prayerful state. The reason our earliest memory of music is so profound is because as infants or young children, our hearts are open. We have not yet developed the defenses that protect our hearts from hurt, nor have we developed a strong ego that pushes forward with its own interests, ignoring the still, small voice of our Essential Musical Intelligence.

According to the teachings of Eastern mysticism, the heart is the seat of the soul, and the soul is the link between spirit and personality. Spirit expresses itself in the form of emotional energy that is colored by the dynamics of specific archetypal issues that we grapple with at a given stage of our development. Emotions are associated with movement (e-motion). They can propel us toward greater feelings of self-worth, creative expression, and harmonious relationships, or lead us to self-doubt, suffering, and destruction. At the level of the heart chakra, we begin to discriminate between emotions that are life giving and emotions that are depleting. As we open to the music of the heart, we are compelled to act out of love and compassion in our dealings with ourselves and others; we recognize that the most powerful energy we possess is love.

In most spiritual traditions throughout history, music has

been used as a way to awaken and purify the heart. According to the *I Ching,* the Chinese Book of Changes, "music has power to ease tension within the heart and to loosen the grip of obscure emotions." The ancient Chinese sages who authored the *I Ching* equated music with enthusiasm:

> The enthusiasm of the heart expresses itself involuntarily in a burst of song, in dance and rhythmic movements of the body. From immemorial times the inspiring effect of the invisible sound that moves all hearts and draws them together has mystified mankind.[2]

In the Sufi tradition, also known as "the path of the heart," surrendering oneself to the practice of devotional music is believed to be the most direct path to enlightenment. The Sufis use song, poetry, and improvisation to passionately express and transform their feelings into spiritual ecstasy as part of their daily ritual of worship. A poem by the much-loved Sufi poet, Kabir, as translated by Robert Bly, demonstrates this sublime reality better than prose:

> The flute of interior time is played whether we
>   hear it or not;
> What we mean by "love" is its sound coming in.
> When love hits the farthest edge of excess, it reaches
>   a wisdom.
> And the fragrance of that knowledge!
> It penetrates our thick bodies,
> it goes through walls—
> Its network of notes has a structure as if a million
>   suns were arranged inside.
> This tune has truth in it.
> Where else have you heard a sound like this?[3]

Center Yourself Through Poetry

Poetry and music are intimately related; they both express, through rhythm and melody, the precious logic of the heart, an incredible source of healing. Take a few moments now to be still. When you are ready, jot down some of your reactions to the preceding poem as a way to center yourself in the witnessing/listening stance of your essential musical intelligence. Notice any changes in your somatic state or mood. Can you let yourself sink more deeply into the wisdom of the heart right now and allow it to guide you? Give yourself time to appreciate this process. In surrendering to the gentle guidance of your intuitive wisdom, you activate the transformational aspect of EMI.

In trying to understand the relationship between intelligence, music, and the heart from a more scientific perspective, I asked my friend Ted, a neuroscientist and classical pianist, what it means when someone plays a piece "by heart." He replied matter-of-factly, "To play from memory." "But," I asked, "shouldn't it really be to play 'by mind' or 'by brain'? What does the heart have to do with memory? Isn't that the domain of the mind?" My scientist friend was stumped. I was compelled to get to the bottom of this conundrum, and after conducting a bit of my own research, I learned that in many traditions, along with being a center for feeling and aesthetic sensibility, the heart is associated with thought and intelligence. In fact, within the framework of traditional Chinese medicine, mind and spirit are intimately related, both being housed within the cave of the heart. In the Japanese language, one word that is used to describe the heart is *kokoro,* which refers to the "mind of the heart."

Current neuropsychological research indicates that the heart has its own independent nervous system, which is actually referred to as "the brain in the heart." According to Doc Childre and Howard Martin, authors of *The Heartmath Solution,* "The heart's intrinsic brain and nervous system relay information back to the brain in the cranium, creating a two-way communication system between heart and brain. The signals sent from the heart to the brain affect many areas and functions in the amygdala, the thalamus, and the cortex."[4]

The amygdala, an almond-shaped structure deep in the limbic system of the brain, specializes in processing strong emotional memories. As we know, music is a perfect container for strong emotions; thus, the heart-brain-music connection. But how did we musicians who have been playing by heart all these years *know* that? Suffice to say that the heart is an important nodal point for Essential Musical Intelligence.

The Voice of EMI

Through opening your heart to the music of your soul, you can pave the way to an even deeper personal relationship with your Essential Musical Intelligence. This relationship manifests itself through the throat chakra, your most vital center for engaging with EMI. When centered in the consciousness of the throat chakra, you open yourself to receiving nurturance, not only physically, through the food you eat and the air that you breathe, but spiritually through your direct relationship with one or more of the glorious forms of Absolute Being. Take a moment now to recall a time when you had the experience of being literally filled up with feelings of joy, awe, and wonder related to some extraordinary (or sometimes quite ordinary) occurrence in your life. Perhaps you have had this kind of peak experience while deeply engaged in creating art (sculpture, music, dance, poetry), or communing with nature (witnessing a brilliant sunset, playing with your new puppy), or during periods of heartfelt prayer or spiritual practice. Often just listening to a few bars of a patriotic song or literally stopping to smell the roses on the way to work can evoke the sensation of awe that reminds us of a reality far greater than what we perceive with our five senses. The word *awe* is associated with childlike innocence and wonder and is itself a breathing sound that seems to express the act of taking in—*in-spir-ation*—breathing in spirit. This receptivity to the life of spirit is the keynote of the throat chakra and the true power behind your Essential Musical Intelligence. At the level of the throat chakra, you naturally open to the innocence of the divine child within and consequently release attachments that block your experience of receiving nurturance (love, harmony, and beauty) from a higher source.

In addition to opening to peak experiences as a way to connect with the consciousness of the throat chakra, many people experience this shift when they are caught in the throes of personal crisis or illness. Often physically or emotionally challenged individuals spontaneously connect with Absolute Being when they have exhausted their ego reserves and are forced to surrender their will to that of a higher power. Through "letting go and letting God," these people often experience profound personal and spiritual transformation that can lead to the healing of their deepest wounds.

Kathy, for example, had suffered from chronic fatigue syndrome for many years. She did everything in her power to overcome the disease: expert medical evaluations, vitamins and supplements, exercise, psychotherapy, and prayer. When I met her, she was barely able to function. She had always loved music, however, so she decided as a last resort to try a few music imagery sessions to connect more deeply with her inner world.

Over the span of five sessions, Kathy began to relive horrifying memories of sexual abuse by her father when she was a child. She spent a year processing the traumatic feelings associated with these events. During this time, her fatigue dramatically diminished. Nevertheless, Kathy was overwhelmed by the emotions related to the abuse, and sometimes felt suicidal.

One day during a particularly painful music-therapy session, Kathy leaned back in her chair with her chin tilted up, eyes closed, and began to hum. The hum came from deep within and filled the space around us. It seemed that she had entered into an altered state. After a few minutes of humming, she opened her eyes and told me that she felt remarkably lighter and free. We both knew that something had shifted. Kathy had connected with the radiance of her throat chakra, which enabled her to recognize her oneness with a force larger than herself and her past afflictions. From that day forward, humming became Kathy's way of remembering that connection. Although she still grappled with painful feelings and choices (like whether to confront her father), she was usually able to hum herself back to balance.

I suggested that she take EMI to the next level and explore this issue through songwriting. Over the next couple of weeks, Kathy wrote the following song, which pulled her out of depression and conferred the power to transform her life:

The Garden

Did you think I would forget? Did you think I didn't feel
the words that stung like poison, the pain that hurt so real?

You led me to your garden, you gave me fruit to eat.
I learned to feel so safe there; then you stole me like a thief.

Father, I was just a child, and everything was new.
And as I grew up stronger, you tried to take that, too.
I played and played and built my world, higher and higher,
Until it all came down, consumed by your fire.

The dark clouds now are lifting, though it's been so many years.
I'll mend a heart that's broken, I've learned to trust my tears.
And now I'm in the garden I've grown with my two hands.
Someday I will let you in—someday, if I can.

Kathy had allowed her Essential Musical Intelligence—through the healing power of her heart and throat chakras—to transform her pain into power. By this point, she had completely recovered from her chronic fatigue and was ready to move into the light of higher consciousness.

By releasing your own egoistic preoccupations at the level of the throat chakra as you practice the exercises that follow, you can increasingly allow yourself to become a clear channel for the expression of your higher self. Because your higher self exists simultaneously within and beyond the mind, it often communicates its wisdom symbolically through sound, music, movement, poetry, and mandalas. Thus, the throat chakra is also the center for imagination and creative expression. You create your own reality through the words that you speak and the artistic forms to which you give birth. The more you direct your creative energies toward the expression of your core truth, the more you activate the transformational aspect of your musical intelligence to create harmony, balance, and healing in your life and in the world around you.

You can connect with the consciousness of the throat chakra through devotional musical activities such as chanting, singing inspirational songs and psalms, songwriting, and vocal and instrumental improvisation. Through spontaneous music making, you can safely express the entire spectrum of emotions, allowing your EMI to transform feelings that are no longer serving you into creative power for change. It is not necessary to be involved in a particular spiritual tradition to open the throat chakra. As you open to the presence of grace in your life, you naturally respond in kind with your own soulful creative expression. Thus, creativity and nurturance are actually two sides of the same coin. When you are being creative, you nurture yourself by receiving guidance from the higher consciousness at the center of your being. In the creative process that provides the framework for utilizing your Essential Musical Intelligence, you open to the source of your most profound healing.

Six Steps to Healing through EMI

The following six steps delineate the healing process of EMI that you can put into practice in your daily life as a way of transforming pain and negativity into increasingly deeper levels of creativity and personal power.

1. **Identify the problem.** Learn to recognize dissonance in your body or mind that may be causing physical or emotional pain or limiting your creative expression. To do this, you must activate the witnessing stance and practice mindfulness: tuning into your thoughts and feelings at regular intervals throughout the day and taking the time to reflect on pain and stuckness instead

of pushing them away. Once you can identify the problem—you are fuming with rage, stuck in a horrendous traffic jam, late for an important meeting—then you can call on EMI to provide a healthy solution.

2. **Remember your true worth**. You are precious and infinitely loved. This is a difficult step for many people, particularly if you have experienced early abuse, abandonment, or trauma. You may feel like you don't matter and consequently relinquish your power and play the victim role. It is so important to realize that, regardless of what happened to you in the past, *you do matter*. Health, harmony, happiness, and abundance are your natural birthright. Tuning into the feeling that you are loved no matter what happens is wonderfully soothing and can instantly defuse the fear and tension of unmanageable situations (like the above traffic jam). In activating this step, it is most helpful to actually remember a specific time when you felt that you were loved unconditionally. Allow this memory and the associated feelings of safety, security, and self-worth to become deeply anchored within you.

3. **Become proactive**. Empower yourself to take responsibility for your own life. Know that although you cannot always prevent or change negative situations (like the traffic jam), you can call upon the creative power of your musical intelligence to help you to transform maladaptive reactions (rage, tension, self-destructive behaviors) to difficult situations. These reactions are ego oriented and, consequently, fear-based; they originate in

the part of the mind that is unable to see the whole picture. Asking for help from your EMI initiates the switch into a more holistic frame of consciousness.

4. **Connect with your throat chakra.** Bring your attention to your throat center and focus your breathing there for a few moments. As this area becomes more energized, imagine that your center of receptivity and expression is opening and expanding. Allow yourself to surrender to the transformational power of EMI as it offers you a musical solution to your problem.
5. **Express yourself.** You *will* receive a musical solution if you allow yourself to hold the tension and listen for your Essential Musical Intelligence. In dealing with a traffic jam, for example, you may be drawn to make up a funny limerick about the situation or to sing your most centering Buddhist chant. Or you may simply pop your hippest James Brown tape into the cassette player, turn up the volume, and channel that rage into a funky rendition of "I Feel Good." In the chapters to come, you will be given numerous specially designed musical exercises to awaken the transformational power of your EMI. Give yourself up to whatever musical idea comes until you begin to feel a significant shift in consciousness.
6. **Give thanks.** When you feel more centered and whole (perhaps even joyful), acknowledge yourself for being proactive and sincerely give thanks to your EMI for its presence in your life and the unlimited possibilities that it offers for healing.

You may liken this six-step transformational process to other stress-management techniques that you have tried in the past. What makes this process unique, however, is that through using music and sound to explore areas of dissonance, you are working directly with the energy of the negative feeling state, engaging it through the creative process of musical expression and allowing your Essential Musical Intelligence (the intuitive wisdom of your higher self) to transform it into a more desirable harmonic state of being. I liken this transformational process to the ancient mystical practice of alchemy, with music and sound as the *prima materia* (or mercuric energy) that turns the proverbial lead of our limited selves into the gold of the awakened self.

As you begin to practice these steps on a regular basis, the process of engaging with EMI eventually becomes more automatic. Before you know it, you will be conditioned to use EMI to root out and harmonize both internal and external dissonance without much conscious effort. Once you have established an ongoing relationship with your Essential Musical Intelligence, it is then important to work systematically, using EMI to awaken, purify, and empower the five levels of consciousness (more about this in the next chapter) that compose the whole of your being, so that all the parts of your self are working together in alignment with a single goal—to sound the music of love. It is only in this state of coherence among the different levels of consciousness that deep and lasting healing can occur. In the following chapters you will learn a number of music and sound techniques to assist you in purifying each level so that the light of your higher self shines through, making all things like itself: perfect.

Chapter Two

*M*usic *of the* *B*ody

O Music,
In your depths we deposit our hearts and souls;
You have taught us to see with our ears
And to hear with our hearts.
—Kahlil Gibran[1]

In order to reach optimal levels of health and wholeness through the six-step process of activating your Essential Musical Intelligence, it is important for you to have experiential knowledge of and access to all aspects of your being. According to yoga science and philosophy, there are five levels of functioning that span the entire spectrum of human consciousness. From the grossest to the most refined, they include the **physical body**, the **energy/breath body**, the **mind**, the **intuition/intellect**, and the level of **bliss.** These levels are also known as *sheaths* in the yoga tradition, since the more evolved level is conceptualized as existing within. They form a continuum that is the basis for all growth and evolution.[2]

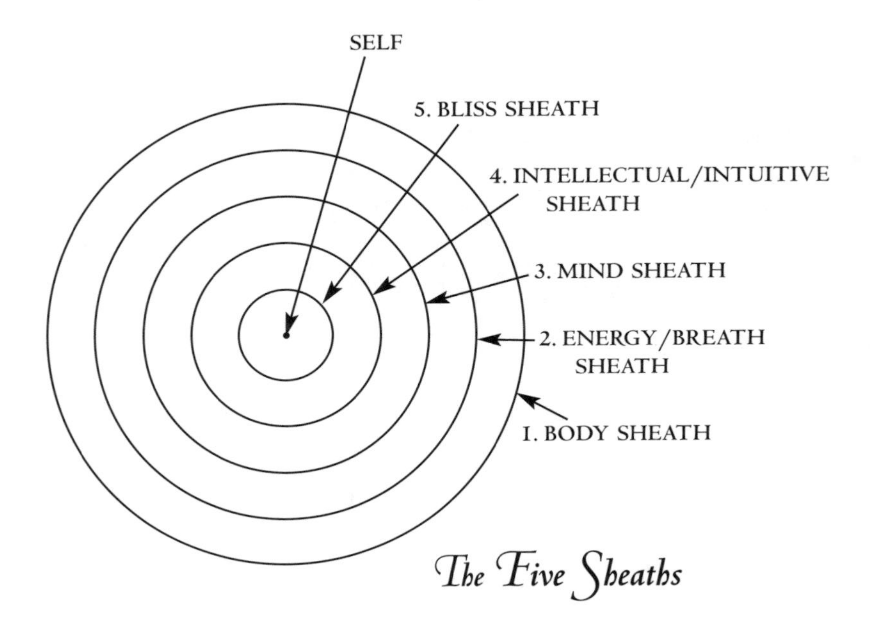

The Five Sheaths

As you will learn in the ensuing chapters, these five levels of being comprise an interactive system, the purpose of which is to create the inner and outer balance that fosters your highest mastery. For example, the energy/breath level gives life to the physical body. The permutations of mind affect the vitality of the energy/breath level. The intellect/intuition level (in its discriminative capacity) empowers the functioning of the mind. Finally, the level of bliss (associated with passive volition) allows you to surrender to the wisdom of the intellect/intuition. Essential Musical Intelligence is like a deep river that runs through and connects each level. When activated, EMI fills in all the dark spaces of your consciousness with the light of spirit or self—your true nature. Thus, the five levels of being comprise a beautiful system of profound intelligence that provides a perfect framework for integrating the six-step healing process of EMI into every dimension of your life.

The Body as Container and Vehicle

We begin at the grossest level of consciousness, the physical body, which is composed of millions of cells that give form to all our bodily structures. These include our bones, muscles, glands, nerves, blood, and other fluids. It is at this level of being that we tend to focus most of our attention. Yet, how many of us truly feel comfortable in our bodies? Most of us feel some pain, stiffness, tension, or dullness in one or more areas of our bodies. According to recent developments in the field of psychoneuroimmunology, the mind is not located solely in the brain; consciousness permeates the entire body. Our bodies reflects the sum total of all our thoughts, attitudes, beliefs, and feelings. If there is constriction in the mind, there will be tension in the body. When we repress or dissociate feelings, the energy of those feelings finds expression somewhere in the body, usually in the form of pain or disease. If we believe that we are unhealthy, weak, or uncoordinated, our bodies will comply.[3]

Along with thoughts and feelings, the body is also the container for higher functions of consciousness, which include intuition (that gut feeling of certainty that you know what is going to happen) and the blissful feelings that manifest physically in chills that run up and down your spine when you surrender to peak experiences. In its most sublime role, the body provides a sacred abode for the life of the soul and can ultimately assist the soul in attaining liberation from the bondage of ignorance and worldly attachment.

The body is also the vehicle for musical expression. Without our bodies, as we learned from Hafiz' story, we would not be able to perceive or create music. (The only reason the angels incarnated into human form, according to Hafiz, was to experience music.) Hafiz' story also implies that the body *is* music, a concept that has recently been confirmed by science. The atoms that form the cells that make up our bodies contain electrons that are in constant motion and that therefore radiate electromagnetic waves. These waves are measurable as frequencies that vary according to the particular body structure. In his book, *The Healing Forces of Music*, Randall McClellan writes:

> Cells whose natural frequency rates are the same combine to form the various structures and systems that are an integral feature of our physical existence. Each structure is a harmonic of the cells through which it is formed and maintained. It may be said, then, that sound creates the structures of our bodies.[4]

Because of the vibratory nature of the body, music has been used from time immemorial as a therapeutic tool to regulate the inner workings of the body. Contemporary music therapy research indicates that music can harmonize and balance all of the rhythms of our bodies, including heart rate, breath, blood pressure, brain-wave frequencies, and the primary respiratory rate. Through its influence on the autonomic nervous system, which is directly linked with the emotional brain centers, music has a salutary effect on immune and hormonal systems as well.[5,6,7]

The body is energetically the most dense of all the levels of human functioning as well as the vehicle for expression of higher consciousness. Therefore, it is most important from the perspective of healing to work with your body in achieving a sense of harmony, balance, and serenity before you attempt to engage the more refined levels. The most efficient way to achieve this state of somatic equilibrium is through music. Relaxing to music helps you to transform stressful states that can otherwise lead to physical malaise.

Musical Relaxation Response

Reserve about thirty minutes. Choose a piece of music that you find soothing, such as Bach's "Air on the G String," Pachelbel's Canon in D, or a favorite piece of sacred or new-age music. Dim the lights, find a comfortable place to sit or lie where you will not be disturbed and turn on the music. Consciously use your breath to let go of tension and allow yourself to completely relax into the music. If you are a visual person, you may be aware of certain images that are evoked by the music. The areas for processing music in the brain are intimately connected to the visual, kinesthetic, olfactory, and emotional brain centers. Let your imagination be stimulated by the music and immerse yourself in the healing images, feelings, and sensations. When the music is over, gently stretch your body. Slowly return to normal consciousness, bringing with you any insights, images, or feelings that may add to your experience of harmony and well-being.

How does listening to music actually transform stress? Let us first define stress as a recurring emotional imbalance resulting in the daily wear and tear on the body that leads to dysfunction and debilitation. The following examples of potentially stressful life situations are probably all too familiar to you: fear of being evaluated during auditions, job interviews, and blind dates, making a mistake during a performance (which could include air traffic controllers as well as musical performers); asking for what you want; getting what you want; losing what you value; fear associated with being stuck in an unmanageable situation, such as a stalled elevator or a difficult relationship; and the experience of having time to kill or no time to lose.

The emotional imbalance triggered by a stressful situation directly affects the functioning of the *autonomic nervous system* (ANS), the part of the nervous system over which we have virtually no direct voluntary control. There are two complementary branches of the ANS that, when working together, create a sense of homeostasis in the mind-body. The *sympathetic nervous system* is associated with emergency situations and arousal. It gives you energy for self-preservation and allows you to get things done. It is also associated with the analytical and sequential functioning of the left-brain hemisphere. When we speak of the fight-or-flight reaction, it is the sympathetic nervous system that becomes activated when we perceive that we are being threatened in some way. Physiological symptoms of sympathetic activation include an increase in heart rate as the heart pumps more blood to the extremities. Blood pressure thus increases, muscles tense in preparation for the concentrated effort to come, digestion decreases so that more energy is available for movement, the mouth becomes dry, organs of elimination are activated to release wastes in order to make the body lighter, and breathing becomes more rapid and shallow.[8]

The complement to the sympathetic arm of the ANS is called the *parasympathetic nervous system.* Its function is to promote inhibition, rest, and pleasurable activity. When the parasympathetic system is activated, your heart rate, breathing, and blood pressure slow down, digestion is activated, muscles relax, and general rehabilitation of the body ensues.

When you experience stress, there is usually an overactivation of the sympathetic arm of the ANS. You are rooted in the fight-or-flight mode and cut off from your Essential Musical

Intelligence. You can learn to transform fight-or-flight responses with stay-and-play activities, such as the Musical Relaxation Response exercise. Listening to soothing music activates the parasympathetic nervous system, which is also associated with the right hemisphere of the brain, the more receptive, integrative, being aspect of consciousness. As your breathing is entrained by the pulse of the music, a feeling of expansiveness ensues; images and emotions are activated and released. You may feel loved and supported by the warmth and holding inherent in the music itself. The irritations caused by daily hassles melt into light as you allow the music to remind you of your true identity.

The Musical Relaxation Response exercise has also been shown to have a positive effect on immunity. Researchers have found that when we are under significant stress, the body produces large amounts of the hormone cortisol, which can weaken the immune system. Listening to soothing, uplifting music in a relaxed state reduces the amount of cortisol in the bloodstream and increases production of specific antibodies that fortify the immune system[9] and protect against infection and disease.

Playing music can also have a salutary effect on the immune system. Ever since I can remember, whenever I notice that I might be coming down with something, my Essential Musical Intelligence naturally signals that it is time to go to the piano. There I let go of my cares and worries and lose myself in musical reveries. I can feel my energy returning as I engage with the music, and more often than not, I escape illness. It is my guess that the feelings of reverence, joy, and gratitude that emerge while I play must have a positive effect on my immune system. This guess has now been confirmed by recent scientific research indicating that positive emotions increase immune responsiveness.

Along these same lines, drumming has a powerful effect on the immune system. Results of a recent groundbreaking study indicate that therapeutic drumming enhances the activity of natural killer cells, the cellular immunity components responsible for seeking out and destroying cancer cells and viruses in healthy individuals. The subjects of the study were nonmusicians who engaged in drumming as a way of releasing tension, expressing themselves in a comfortable group environment, and simply having fun.[10] The results of this study have important implications for prevention of numerous disease processes, including cancer.

Recreational drumming has become quite popular over the last several years. Drumming circles span a wide range of purposes and locales from creativity enhancement in executive boardrooms on Madison Avenue, to full-moon celebrations with hundreds of drummers in Central Park. The secret is out! Drumming is a powerful way of getting in touch with the deep instinctual energies of the body. It is a safe medium for expressing these energies, for letting go of inhibitions, and ultimately allowing the mind-body to experience its innate creativity. At a more subtle level, however, I believe that perhaps it is not the drumming itself, but the state that you achieve during drumming. George Leonard, in his book, *The Silent Pulse,* beautifully expresses this concept.

> At the heart of each of us, whatever our imperfections, there exists a silent pulse of perfect rhythm, a complex of wave forms and resonances, which is absolutely individual and unique, and yet which connects us to everything in the universe. The act of getting in touch with this pulse can transform our personal experience and in some way alter the world around us.[11]

Silent Pulse

You can connect with this silent pulse by exploring your natural inner rhythms through recreational drumming. Choose a drum (either a frame drum or a larger standing drum) made of natural materials (dried animal skin, wood, ceramic, or metal). Spend some time communing with your drum, feeling its vibration, getting a sense of its history, before you begin to play. Now, allow yourself to connect with your Essential Musical Intelligence as you listen to the subtle rhythms of your heartbeat. Once you connect with your own core rhythm, you may want to play it (with your hands or a mallet) on your drum, feeling the subtle pulse moving through your body and out through your hands, connecting with the skin of the drum. Repeat your core rhythm over and over until you feel completely in sync with your body and the drum. When you are ready, surrender to your EMI and let the music guide you. Be aware of specific feelings and images that emerge while playing. When your improvisation is complete, allow yourself to sit quietly and experience the deep sense of safety and security of the silent pulse. You may want to process this experience in your journal once the music is over. This exercise also works well in group situations, where you can connect with your unique inner pulse and at the same time realize your unity with the silent pulse of everyone else in your group.

Aside from practicing musical stress-reduction/immune enhancement techniques as part of your daily wellness routine at home, you can also engage your EMI to create a healthy musical environment within the workplace.

Several years ago I received a phone call from a personal trainer. His client, Leo, chairman of the board of a major securities firm, was suffering from dangerously high blood pressure. Noting that his client was an avid audiophile, the trainer wanted to see if the healing power of music could help Leo to lower his blood pressure. I advised him to purchase a CD player that could hold at least five discs. I gathered up about twenty CDs of my favorite healing music and made a house call.

I arrived at about ten o'clock on Monday morning to find the chairman's office hopping. Phones rang, TVs and radios blared, and brokers stormed in and out, making what seemed to me life-and-death decisions at a moment's notice. I had to make a special request for a few minutes of Leo's time so that he could listen to some of the music I had brought. We were interrupted several times, but finally we chose five CDs that Leo could live with for the next couple of weeks. The music included selections from *Playing with Fire, The Celtic Fiddle Collection,* Brian Eno's *Music for Airports,* Janalea Hoffman's *Deep Daydreams,* and Kolbialka's *Velvet Dreams.* I programmed the CD player using the iso (meaning "same") principle. This technique protects the client against shock or irritation by first using music that matches his mood and then moving on to music that eases him into a more desirable feeling state. The first piece I chose for Leo was a rather high-pitched, springy reel from *The Celtic Fiddle Collection* titled "Reel Beatrice," followed by several other reels and jigs, to match Leo's high-strung nature and to mirror his fiery heart rhythms. I then added progressively more relaxing (but not too relaxing) pieces to the mix to entrain Leo's consciousness to an optimal state of focused relaxation. (The scientific theory of entrainment suggests that the order and coherence of certain kinds of music can energetically pull an unbalanced individual into rhythmic and harmonic resonance with it. Musical entrainment is a passive yet powerful phenomenon that often occurs without conscious awareness.) Leo and I also went over some basic breathing and relaxation exercises to use along with the music whenever he felt his blood pressure rising.

Dramatic changes in the dynamics of Leo's office occurred with the music playing for just fifteen minutes. These changes confirmed the validity of the entrainment concept. Partners would race in, fists clenched and anxious with some acute problem, then walk out a few minutes later with soft smiles on their faces. Leo would grab the constantly ringing phone, initially spitting out words in his usual staccato style; then, after a moment of tuning into the music, he would lean back in his chair and modulate his voice to match the pulse of the music. The subliminal effect of the music provided a higher, more refined rhythm that entrained the chairman and his cohorts to the vibration of their Essential Musical Intelligence—harmony, order, and beauty.

Leo's trainer called me later that day to report that Leo's blood pressure had returned to normal. He believed that the music was definitely the dependent variable. He called again at the end of the work week and confirmed that Leo had been able to maintain normal blood pressure throughout the week, and that he also noticed positive changes in many of the employees who worked closely with Leo. While tuning into the music, Leo and his colleagues were able to move from arousal to rest in a rhythmic flow throughout the day. This flow state is the optimal condition for a healthy and creative body and mind.

If you suffer from unavoidable stress at work, you can create your own healing environment to assist you in connecting with your Essential Musical Intelligence throughout the day. The key to using music for entrainment is to select music that creates a mood conducive to focusing, creating, and carrying out work that needs to be done.

EMI in the Workplace

Go through your CD collection and select about twenty pieces of music that you would feel comfortable listening to as a backdrop to your daily work routine. I suggest instrumental music, as music with lyrics can be emotionally arousing and thus distracting.

After you have selected your music, divide it into two general categories—stimulating music and soothing music. Using the iso principle, program your CD player upon arriving at work with several pieces that match your mood and basic temperament. Then choose a number of pieces that will move you in the direction of greater clarity, energy, peace, and productivity. Adjust the volume so that the music is barely audible yet still capable of affecting the ambience of your work space. I like to start with mellow jazz; for example, a medley of cuts from the classic Miles Davis album, *Kind of Blue,* followed by a gradual shift into the slow movements from music by my favorite baroque composers, Handel, Bach, and Vivaldi, whom I find especially relaxing and balancing. I may end the series with traditional Sufi music, which is wonderfully invigorating and inspirational. Depending upon your needs, your entrainment music program may last from one to two hours and can be repeated throughout the day as it is or altered to accommodate natural shifts in your energy, mood, and work demands.

Transforming Pain Through EMI

Swiss scientist Hans Jenny suggests that sound in a multitude of frequencies actually gives form to our physical bodies. Jenny discovered that different tones produce distinct archetypal patterns when vibrated through a sound oscillator into iron filings, liquid, or powder media. In addition, using a tonoscope that produces a picture of the sound pattern, Jenny demonstrated that the human voice can also be made visible. He found that different vowels produced characteristic visual patterns—in other

The pattern of sound of the vowel "Ah" as produced through a tonoscope

words, form. You can literally see the spectrum of the sounds. It is interesting to note that when the tone ceases, the visual pattern disappears.[12] Jenny's research seems to confirm the Eastern mystical premise that vibration is the essence of all life. Perhaps it also explains T. S. Eliot's observation that "you are the music while the music lasts." Our inner music is the framework for the constantly changing mandalas (matter) that we call our bodies.

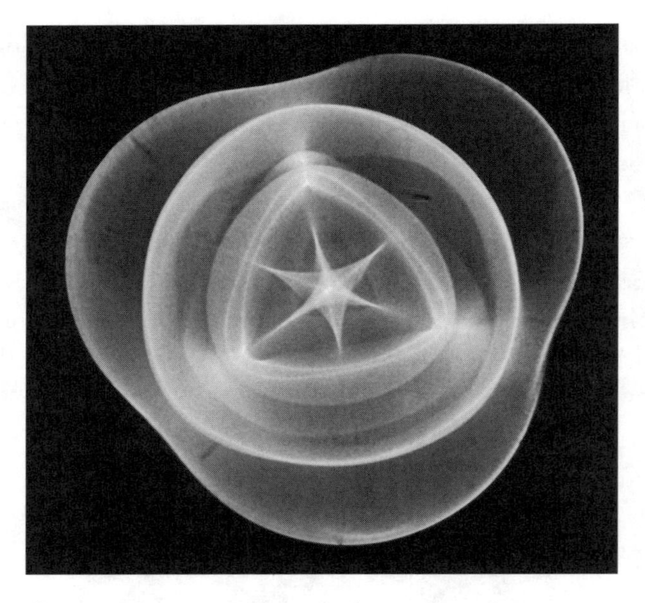

"A trigonal configuration is predominant in this figure . . . While the tone persists, the phenomenon continues in motion as a total situation perpetually seeking wholeness."

If the body is actually a vibrating field of energy—a living composition, if you will—then pain, stiffness, and numbness can be seen as musical roadblocks, a damming up of the flow of life energy, perhaps even a crystallization of energy—zero movement. The voice is the main instrument for sound production in the body. It is intimately linked with the breath, which is continually affected by both fleeting and hard-wired thoughts and feelings. The voice is also the creative center of your being, where deep healing and transformation are set into motion through the power of the "word," meaning vibrational essence. Using your voice as a channel for creative sound making, you can instantly connect with your Essential Musical Intelligence. As you become more familiar with your inner landscapes, you can use your voice to pinpoint physical blockages and focus intentional sound like a laser beam directly into blocked areas, melting frozen patterns of energy with the harmonics of solar light.

What exactly makes up these frozen energy patterns? According to yoga science and recent psychophysiological research, pain can be perceived as a nonverbal form of communication stemming from physical or emotional trauma.[13] If you are shocked or hurt in some way and unable to process the experience, the memories and feelings related to the trauma are often dissociated and stored in the body. The pain that eventually surfaces in this part of the body is actually a request that the light of consciousness be directed toward it in a way that will permit it to play out its unresolved and dissociated conflicts.

One of my first music-therapy clients was a forty-three-year-old woman who had been paralyzed from the waist down after a brutal attack by one of her students in a school for developmentally delayed children where she had taught for eleven years. Susan had received medical evaluations from a variety of clinicians, none of whom could help her. My approach, which combined sound therapy with hands-on body work using the five-element system, was Susan's last resort. As I palpated several points along her body associated with the five elements (earth, water, fire, air, and ether), I soon realized that ether, associated with the throat chakra, was particularly weak. I found a point near the base of Susan's skull that was very tender and, with her permission, applied some pressure while simultaneously sounding a tone to facilitate the release of blocked energy. After a minute or so, I could feel some energy beginning to move under my fingers. Suddenly, Susan began to shake uncontrollably. She started gasping for air, and then the floodgates opened. Susan wailed and sobbed for about ten minutes. As she cried, I could see the energy returning to her pelvis and legs. Now they too were shaking.

When Susan finally calmed down and her breathing returned to normal, she told me that she had just relived the entire attack of nearly five years before. She said that the tone I made was like a key that unlocked the door to memories and feelings that had been split off and buried for so long. She then described what had taken place on that fateful day. Afterward, I was curious to see if perhaps Susan could stand and maybe even walk a bit. She was extremely resistant at first, but as she realized that she actually felt sensations in her legs that she hadn't felt in years, she attempted to swing herself to an upright position on the treatment table, then gradually ease herself down to a standing position. She stood for a few seconds and then collapsed in joyful realization that her days of living like an invalid were soon to be over. (Susan eventually regained her mobility.)

After that session with Susan, I began to experiment with toning in my work with clients who had intractable pain and other kinds of numbness and paralysis. Time and time again I found that combining sound with physical manipulation was quite effective. It was even more effective when the client toned along with me.

In trying to understand from a psychophysiological perspective how creating particular sounds could help to release dissociated feelings and memories stored in the physical body, I was drawn to Ernest Rossi's book, *The Psychobiology of Mind-Body Healing.* According to Rossi, the shock of a traumatic experience often sends an individual into a dissociative trance state, which is actually a natural defense against the horror of the moment. Memories acquired during the trance state are forgotten in the awake state, but available once again when a trance is reinduced.[14] It is my hypothesis that sound making creates a trancelike environment and that the trance, along with the pain associated with physical manipulation—perhaps even the specific sound frequency—triggers the memory of the trauma and allows the client to process in a safe context the overwhelming thoughts and feelings associated with the experience.

Toning functions as a catalyst for emotional release, a way of allowing a "dis-eased" part of the mind-body to safely express itself. The term *toning* was coined by the late pioneer of sound healing, Laurel Keyes, in her groundbreaking book of the same title. Keyes pointed out that all living beings make sound to release tension or increase strength.[15] This reflex is hardwired into the instinctual centers of the brain. Unfortunately, the expression of natural sounds is taboo in many so-called civilized cultures today. We learn to cover our mouths when we laugh, yawning is discouraged, and some people even suppress the sneeze.

Still, sound making is a way for the instinctual parts of our consciousness, which are often hidden or repressed, to directly communicate their healing message through the body. For instance, groaning is a powerful way to release deep tensions and frustrations held within the body. The growl is also a way to get in touch with your animal nature. There was a period in my life when I allowed myself to wake up each morning with a growl, not necessarily an angry growl, but more like the roar of a lioness. I can't tell you how energizing this was for me. My whole body tingled, and I felt more alert and motivated than I ever had before. Allowing yourself to groan in the shower is another delightful way to release stress and strain—and it's fun, too!

Another way to get in touch with natural sounds is to play with making other animal sounds, sounds of nature, and industrial sounds and rhythms. Through your own sound making you can explore the richness of the music of life that is all about you. You may also want to explore making expressive human sounds such as sighing, crying, laughing, popping, cooing, etc. Be aware of where you may feel these sounds vibrating in your body and also of any emotional reactions to specific sounds. Once you feel comfortable with creating natural sounds, you can use toning to facilitate healing in a particular part of your body.

The Healing Tone

This exercise can be done in a standing, seated, or supine position. To start the toning process, ground, center, and relax your mind-body. You may want to close your eyes in order to create the sensation of moving more deeply within. When you are ready, bring your full attention to the area of pain or numbness in the body and listen for a sound or tone. As you center your consciousness fully in that area, images and spontaneous movements may emerge along with the tone that can facilitate a deeper state of connection. Allow yourself to incorporate them into your healing process.

You may feel foolish or even embarrassed to give full voice to the emerging sound, but if you can, just let go of these judgments. Take a deep breath and sound the tone for the entire length of your exhalation. The actual pitch that you hear can be intoned on any vowel sound, AYE, EE, EYE, OH, OO, or AH. You may also intuit a certain rhythm along with the tone. Feel free to repeat this rhythm while you are toning. Continue toning on your out breaths, imagining the sound and rhythm releasing blocked energy and allowing a new sense of freedom of movement and expression. You may feel tingling as energy begins to flow into the blocked area. Sometimes waves of emotion are unleashed as the dissociated memories at the root of the energy block begin to surface. Continue to tone as long as you feel comfortable and safe.

When you have completed the toning exercise, write about your experience in your Music and Sound Awareness Journal. This is also a good time to create healing affirmations that attest to your worthiness and your desire to be healthy and whole. When you tune into your innate healing ability through the process of toning, you let go of the limitations of the rational mind and allow the improvisational aspect of your Essential Musical Intelligence to lead you toward greater self-awareness, integration, and wholeness.

Over the years, many of my students have used toning in dealing with health issues. One student, Rita, was plagued with recurring migraines. She had tried both conventional drug therapy and alternative treatments like acupuncture and biofeedback, but neither modality afforded lasting relief. She wanted to use music to defuse the pain of her migraines and explore any underlying emotional causes. After practicing the healing-tone exercise for several weeks, Rita found herself in the grip of a burgeoning migraine. She was determined to put her toning exercise to the test. Once her initial anger and irritation subsided, Rita was able to go within and listen for the "voice" of her migraine. She took a few moments to relax and center herself and then proceeded to tone a high-pitched EE sound, which she sensed in the middle of her forehead. This, she believed, was the sound of her migraine. As she explored this sound and moved it around the inside of her skull, she gradually lowered the pitch from high EE down to a low OH sound in her belly. She imagined that a lavender cross was being drawn from her forehead down to and across her chest, and then down to her belly. There she felt a wave of comfort and she heaved a deep sigh. She played with the OH sound for a while and soon realized that her migraine had subsided.

I asked Rita if she had any understanding of what had occurred. Rita told me that the EE sound was a scream trapped inside her head related to her ambivalence toward her current work situation. She was able to release this scream through the toning exercise, which also led her to a place of power and earthiness in her belly where she discovered the OH sound. I suggested that she continue to experiment with the OH sound to see if it could lead her to more insights about the kind of work that would be truly fulfilling. Rita eventually left her job and became a music therapist!

As your physical body becomes more healthy and whole through the process of toning, you may want to practice a daily prevention-oriented sound exercise to create a deeper level of balance and harmony. The following exercise was taught to me by the renowned Sufi teacher and musician, Pir Vilayat Khan, as way to balance the five vital elements—earth, water, fire, air, and ether—that sustain and nourish the physical body.[16]

Sounding the Five Elements

Find a comfortable seated position, keeping your spine straight, in a space where you will not be disturbed for at least twenty minutes. Systematically ground, center, and relax. Turn your focus inward and visualize the energy at the base of your spine. The earth element is associated with this region of the body. Breathing in and out through the nose, imagine the magnetism of the earth rising up to give you life, support, and sustenance. When you are ready, allow yourself to tone the sound of the earth element, humming the lowest-pitched sound you can muster from the depths of your being. If you have ever heard the Gyuto Tantric monks chanting, the sound of the earth element is quite similar to this almost subsonic utterance.

Next, bring your concentration to the area an inch or two below the navel, the center of the water element. Breathe in through the nose and out through the mouth as you visualize water flowing throughout your entire being. You may imagine a river, a waterfall, a babbling brook, or any other moving body of water. Allow the element of water to release any areas of tension and inhibition in the pelvic area and feel the ever-flowing waters giving life to your creative urges. The sound of the water element is OO (as in cool). Breathe in and on your exhalation, vibrate the OO sound directly into the pelvic area. Continue to vibrate this sound on your out breaths for a minute or so.

Enjoy the sensual, soothing, nurturing quality of the water sound.

Next bring your focus to your solar plexus, located between rib cage and navel, the abode of the fire element. Breathe in through the mouth and out through the nose as you visualize fire burning in the hearth of your mind-body. Allow fire to give you the power to let go of all that is inessential in your life and to ignite your inner passion. The sound that most expresses the energy of fire is the syllable HO. Think of Santa Claus with his resounding laugh, "Ho, ho, ho!" Native Americans use HO to powerfully affirm self-expression and identity. You can vibrate the HO sound either in short spurts to ignite the fire center or intone a long HO sound on your exhalations to increase strength and endurance.

Next focus on your heart, the center of the air element. Breathe in and out through the mouth as you visualize the movement of air bringing life, love, and freedom to all. The sound of the air element is AH, vibrated softly into the heart center. Allow yourself to feel the palate in the back of your throat rise as you allow the beautiful AH sound to emerge. Continue to tone the AH sound on your exhalations until your heart is full.

Finally, focus on the throat, the home of the ether element, the infinite space out of which all the other elements are manifested. Breathe a refined breath in and out through the nostrils as you expand your consciousness into the unlimited space within and without. Allow yourself to intone the syllable HU on your exhalation. You may stimulate the center even more if you close your mouth as you tone HU, vibrating your lips and creating subtle overtones which have a purifying effect on the energy system.

Systematically toning the five elements on a daily basis is a wonderful way to connect with your Essential Musical Intelligence and revitalize your entire being. It is also an effective system for self-diagnosis. When you practice this exercise, notice how some of the elemental tones are easier to sound than others. The five elements correspond to specific physical organs: earth is associated with the large intestine, adrenal glands, bones, and other gross matter; water with the sex organs, kidneys, and bodily fluids; fire with the digestive organs; air with the heart and respiratory system; and ether with the throat, thyroid, and thymus glands. If there is a weakness in a particular organ or system of the body, it will probably be reflected in the sound quality and/or the amount of life force expressed in its corresponding elemental sound. Try to spend more time toning into the areas that seem weak or constricted. Be gentle with yourself. In time, you will find your energy becoming more balanced and your body stronger, healthier, and glowing with life.

Music as Anesthesia

Your Essential Musical Intelligence can also be used effectively in dealing with the acute pain associated with physical injury. Music therapy research has shown that people who listen to music before and after surgical operations require less anesthesia and pain medication and recover faster than those people who did not listen to music.[17] Apparently, when we listen to music that is uplifting and emotionally moving, the body reacts by releasing endorphins, our body's natural painkillers.[18] Along with the endorphin effect, listening to music can be a powerful distraction from our intense focus on pounding pain rhythms. Listening to music can actually move us into an altered state, or trance, where we can dissociate from the pain. In this way, music expands our experience of time from the panic state associated with acute pain to the state of timelessness where consciousness unites with the Universal Mind. In this state there is no pain, only infinite peace and quiet.

Another student, Peter, a businessman and amateur jazz musician, relayed this story of how he used his Essential Musical Intelligence in transforming the pain associated with a root canal procedure:

> Not too many things bother me, but when it comes to my teeth, I am a dental phobic. When my dentist discovered a serious infection in one of my molars, he told me that the only way to save the tooth was to do a root canal. Terrified at the thought of the pain involved, I thought about making a tape that would take my mind off the pain and send me into an altered state. I had just finished a rehearsal with my jazz quartet and had recorded the group playing a couple of my tunes. I decided to bring the rehearsal tape to the dentist's office to listen to during the procedure.
>
> Listening to my band talking and playing music together while I sat waiting for the novocaine to kick in was incredible. I felt held by the music and completely lost myself in the experience of listening to the tunes, feeling gratitude to my fellow

bandmates, and letting the sounds wash over me and comfort me in my hour of need. It seemed that hardly any time had gone by when my dentist told me that he had completed the first stage of the root canal.

The key to using music as anesthesia and for pain reduction is to choose music that you connect with very deeply on an emotional level, music that is distracting, all absorbing. Peter's choice of his own music with his own voice and the voices of people that he loved and trusted provided a safe, warm, and loving environment that held his attention and created nurturance at the same time. What kind of music would you choose if you were in a similar situation?

EMI and Childbirth

Many mothers have described the birthing process as one of the most profoundly joyful and excruciatingly painful experiences of their lives. By tapping into your Essential Musical Intelligence, you can use music (both listening and sound making) to transform the pain of labor into a creative, self-nurturing, and joyful experience. Toning in particular is quite helpful in facilitating the release of pain as opposed to the natural inclination to recoil in fear. Creating two separate tapes, one with primarily soothing music and one with dramatic, powerful, energetic music, can be used interchangeably throughout the birthing process, depending on your mood and physical condition.

Singing is also a wonderful way to connect with the baby and with your loved ones during the birthing process. Choose five of your favorite songs that are uplifting, inspiring, and empowering and that you would feel comfortable belting out or whispering during this special time. Write out the lyrics several weeks beforehand and bring a number of copies to share with your loved ones. The act of singing meaningful songs together during such a highly charged emotional experience can instantly relieve anxiety, decrease pain, and create deep spiritual bonds among all involved.

The Musical Diet

Many people say that music is food for the soul, but can it also be sustenance for the physical body? In working with people with eating disorders, I have found that the six-step process of activating EMI works extremely well in transforming maladaptive thoughts, feelings, and desires related to overeating, and in providing deeper levels of nourishment for the hungry body and soul. Here is how you can use EMI to harmonize your relationship with food and eating.

1. Identify the problem. To review, the first step is to activate the witness stance. Once you are in this observational mode, you can use EMI to help you to discriminate emotional hunger from physical hunger. When you are feeling hungry, stop first and ask yourself what you are truly feeling. People who overeat often use hunger to cover up more complex feelings like fear, loneliness, emptiness, and rage. If you eat when you are not really hungry, you will not be totally present because the part of you that feels lonely, fearful, etc., is dissociated. If you are not fully present, you miss out on the psychological nourishment you crave, and you find yourself hungry again in no time.

2. Remember your true worth. You are precious and infinitely loved. When you eat to cover up painful feelings, you are in a state of self-judgment and loathing, unable to acknowledge and honor your feeling states. Remember, every part of you is lovable, not just the parts that look good on the outside. In addition to covering up feelings, overeating may also be a way to express a sense of entitlement—"I can eat as much as I want!" However, underneath those feelings is usually a deep well of deprivation and associated anger.

3. Become proactive. When you are unable to acknowledge and accept painful emotions, you often feel shame and guilt and consequently wall yourself off from others. This is one of the reasons that it is so difficult to transform emotionally based eating patterns: food becomes a substitute for human love. When you call upon your musical intelligence to fill you with your true essence, you are choosing not to abandon yourself. This is the most important step in then being able to ask others for love and support.

4. Connect with your throat chakra. Eating issues are often centered around the emotional dynamics of the throat chakra (nurturance, creativity, longing). When feeling emotion-based hunger, instead of eating, bring your attention to your throat and focus your breathing there for a few moments. Lift yourself out of your downward emotional spiral and trust that your EMI will provide a creative solution to the emotional conflicts underlying your desire to eat.

5. Express yourself. If, through listening to the still, small voice of your EMI, you realize that you are feeling deprived, angry, lonely, or afraid, you can use music—particularly singing—to give voice to the true dynamics of your hunger.

6. Give thanks. When you have successfully used music to center yourself in EMI and find that your emotional hunger pangs have passed, allow yourself to feel gratitude for the ever-present spirit of EMI in your life. Each time you can remember to use this six-step process to transform emotional hunger, you will move closer to your goal of developing healthy, fulfilling eating patterns and, as an added bonus, experience greater levels of life energy, self-esteem, and creativity in the process.

I witnessed an elegant demonstration of the fifth step quite by chance while attending the taping of a cooking show that featured fitness guru Richard Simmons as the celebrity chef. It was a call-in show and Mr. Simmons was busy cooking up a storm and answering questions from interested viewers as he worked. I was quite amused at Simmons' musicality as he interacted with the food, callers, and crew. It seemed that every other sentence was part of a song that he sang in a playful yet serious manner. I approached Simmons after the show and commented on his delightful engagement with singing. He smiled and said that music was his life and that no matter what was going on, he could always depend on singing to lift his spirit.

It seemed to me that Simmons used singing to create a harmonious emotional climate that would serve him in accomplishing what was needed in the moment. To the average person with weight problems, this constant engagement with improvisational singing might seem a bit extreme. However, finding a way to connect with music in the midst of loneliness, depression, and even plain old excitement, is truly the key to transforming emotional overeating. You might use a favorite song, as Liz did in chapter 1, to intervene when your urge to binge is activated. Some of my students find playing simple wind instruments like the tin whistle or recorder quite helpful when dealing with emotional hunger. You can also take a few minutes to listen to your most nurturing piece of music while breathing rhythmically and deeply, centering yourself in the deep aura of self-acceptance that radiates outward from your EMI. As you begin to feel more peaceful and centered, you will eventually be able to perceive your natural hunger cues and will be more apt to "hear" when you are full than when you are eating for emotional reasons.

Consciously engaging EMI to relax, purify, and strengthen the physical body is the first and most important step in facilitating profound healing of body, mind, and spirit. Once the body is relaxed, you can then begin to use EMI to awaken, purify, and strengthen the more subtle breath/energy body that surrounds the physical body. It is this breath/energy body that, in addition to its role of energizing and nurturing the higher levels of being, ultimately provides vital energy to enliven and heal the physical body.

Chapter Three

Music *as* Life Force Energy

Time is breath.
—G. I. Gurdjieff

The breath/energy realm provides a link between the denser material body and the more subtle realm of the mind. According to Sufi master Hazrat Inayat Khan, "The breath is the result of a current [which] runs not only through the body, but also through all the planes of man's existence . . . the current of the whole of nature . . . is the real breath . . . It is the one breath and yet it is many breaths."[1]

Prana, the vital essence of breath which, in the Sanskrit language means "the very life," is the energy that underlies all activity, both physical and mental. From the perspective of Oriental medicine, the Western medical approach of treating disease solely on the cellular level is superficial. Eastern practitioners believe that true healing takes place at a subtler level—that of the energy body, the vehicle of consciousness and mental events. By understanding and working with breath/energy, you can directly affect both mental and physical states.

The energy body is actually the vibrational framework around which the physical body is formed. Imagine Hans Jenny's inert iron filings suddenly coming to life and arranging themselves into archetypal patterns as different tones are vibrated into the metal plate on which they rest. This phenomenon is greatly magnified in the human body. If you could actually see and hear the human energy body, you would be privy to the most amazing constellations of melody, rhythm, light, color, and wave—energetic mandalas in constant motion, fueled by the Great Tone, *Nada Brahma,* the origin of all life. Sound is the audible expression of Spirit, which enlivens every cell of our bodies and all life on the planet. Kirlian photography shows us that even after a piece of a leaf is cut away and discarded, the energetic structure of the leaf still pulses with life. A person who loses a limb still feels discomfort where the body part once existed. Even though the matter component of the limb is absent, the energetic framework still functions.

Your Essential Musical Intelligence is intimately connected with the energy/breath realm. EMI is expressed through the breath in the form of sound, which is, of course, pure vibration. Through working with music and sound, you can become consciously aware of the relationship between breath, energy, and healing. As you become more sensitized to your breath rhythms and the flow of energy through your body, you will realize that most imbalances or blocks to perfect health exist in the energy/breath realm before they are manifested in your body. Becoming aware of how sound affects your breathing and the flow of energy in and through your being, and then using EMI to harmonize and balance your energy system can help prevent energetic blocks from taking root in your body. It is empowering to know that you do not have to get sick in order to begin healing.

You can be present in your radiant self at all times, using your Essential Musical Intelligence to create harmony and balance with every breath you take.

Creative Use of Breath for Enhancing Life Energy and Healing

When you connect with EMI, it is actually the creative aspect of the energy/breath that is being expressed in and through you. The energy/breath level contains the alchemical force that is so powerfully tapped through your heartfelt engagement with music and sound. Thus, EMI provides a conduit for the birth of Spirit, or divine intelligence, into matter. A qualitative difference exists, however, between the birth process at the level of the body as compared to the level of energy/breath. Giving birth to a baby typically requires long periods of labor. The birth of Spirit into matter is another story. When working with the energy/breath body, you must first learn to practice passive volition, the act of consciously letting go and *allowing* energy/breath to enliven you with its transformational healing energies. Only through passive volition can you create a clear space for the intelligence of the soul, which is carried by the breath and expressed through the body, to enliven your being.

The key to developing this new attitude of receptivity and surrender to your Essential Musical Intelligence can be found in your conscious relationship with your own breath. If you practiced the Breath Awareness exercise in chapter 1, you are probably familiar with your own breathing style and rhythms. Breath awareness takes you out of the realm of worrying about the future and fretting about the past and into the pregnant moment of the infinite now. When I asked Rachel, one of my students, how she felt after practicing breath awareness for the first time, she looked at me incredulously and said, "I found myself!" As she observed her breathing, Rachel became attracted to the pause at the end of her exhalations. In that brief pause was the most delicious sense of peace and stillness, a feeling that had apparently eluded her while she was caught in the chaos of daily life.

For most people, the initial experience of observing their breath is not so enlivening. In fact, a number of my students are quick to confess that they don't know how to breathe, or that they breathe incorrectly. For example, when he first practiced breath awareness, Joseph noticed that he favored exhaling over inhaling. When I asked him if he understood why, he said that when he inhaled, he felt like he was "stealing" his breath, that he didn't have the right to take too much. This student, incidentally, had issues around receiving abundance.

Sarah, a film editor who suffered from extreme anxiety and a serious work-related overuse injury, discovered that she breathed primarily in her chest (as opposed to diaphragmatic breathing) and was unable to exhale fully. As she explored her resistance to letting go during her exhalations, a barrage of childhood images flooded her mind. She saw herself as a child of seven taking on the responsibility for her four younger siblings shortly after her father abandoned the family. Sarah remembered her mother as extremely anxious and fragile, often depending on her to keep the household running smoothly. From that time on, Sarah had never been able to rest fully (she was now forty-two years old). She was always hypervigilant, ever the caretaker. When she realized how this compulsion to work hard (which led to her overuse injury) was reflected in her core breathing pattern, she began to sob uncontrollably for the little girl who was never allowed to just be.

As you can see, your relationship with the core of your being is clearly reflected in your habitual breathing patterns. These patterns become internalized early on and determine the quality of your mental and physical health. The good news is that maladaptive breathing patterns can be changed, thereby allowing you to reinstate the full, unimpeded diaphragmatic breathing that you naturally experienced as a small child.

The diaphragm is a dome-shaped muscle that attaches to the lowest two ribs and separates the thoracic cavity from the abdominal cavity. The muscle presses down when you breathe in to allow more air to fill the lungs, and moves up when you exhale, pushing out the stale air. Take a few moments now to experiment with diaphragmatic breathing.

Diaphragmatic Breathing

If you are not familiar with diaphragmatic breathing, lie down on a mat or carpet with one palm on the center of your chest and the other on your abdomen. As you inhale, the lower edge of your rib cage should expand and your abdomen rise; as you exhale, the opposite should happen. There should be relatively little movement in your upper chest. Continue breathing diaphragmatically for five to ten minutes. Practice this exercise twice a day for a month. Use your Music and Sound Awareness Journal to record any physical, mental, and emotional changes that may be related to your new breathing style. Most likely, as diaphragmatic breathing becomes habitual and automatic, you will find it much easier to connect with your Essential Musical Intelligence.

In diaphragmatic breathing, lung expansion is focused on the lower gravity-dependent areas of the lungs where oxygen exchange proceeds more efficiently. In addition to providing the most efficient breathing pattern, the diaphragm, as it contracts, pushes the abdominal organs down and forward. This rhythmical massage promotes improved circulation. Diaphragmatic breathing also brings your center of gravity down to the belly—your power center—where you can disengage from the anxiety and worry associated with chest breathing and begin to feel more secure and grounded. It is only from this deep, centered place that you can get in touch with your gut feelings and the wisdom of EMI as it expresses itself through the body.

The Importance of Rhythmic Breathing

Hazrat Inayat Khan writes that the whole mechanism of the body works by the power of the breath, and every disorder in the mechanism is caused by some irregularity in breathing. He goes on to say that most physicians claim that it is the physical body that causes changes in blood pressure and heart rate, but that mystics know these changes are caused by the breath. Khan believes that the most important factor to be considered in breathing is rhythm.

Take some time today to reflect on your own breath rhythms. Most likely you will find that when you feel impatient and lack endurance, your breath is shallow. Erratic breath rhythms lead to confusion and make you vulnerable to emotional outbursts. You may also notice that you hold your breath, which sometimes occurs when you are concentrating intensely. More often than not, breath holding is a sign of dissociation between mind and body and severely disrupts the flow of energy, leading to confusion, lethargy, and exhaustion.

Breathing rhythmically connects you with the universal pulse of nature, which gives you instant access to your Essential Musical Intelligence. There is a great difference between breathing in a linear style from the level of mind and ego where your breath rhythms constantly fluctuate with external changes and breathing with the universal pulse. When your breath is in sync with the pulse of nature, you have surrendered your will (the limited ego) to that of Absolute Being. You have allowed yourself, no matter what is going on in your life, to rest in the loving arms of the Great Mother and to trust in the reality of divine order.

For example, there is order to the rising and setting of the sun, the changing phases of the moon, the movement of the tides. This pulse exists within us too. Through practicing rhythmic breathing, you can allow yourself to be conscious of its pull and its subtle movement originating in the cave of the heart. You become like a mountain—impenetrable, immovable. You can live fully in the world, yet remain detached. Rhythmic breathing also has a salutary effect on the physical body. When you can allow your exhalation in particular to become deeper and longer, you naturally activate the relaxation response. Breathing deeply and rhythmically reverses the ravages of chronic sympathetic nervous system overdrive (a/k/a stress), naturally balancing out all the rhythms of the body and allowing you to function at peak levels of performance. The following exercise was adapted from the work of noted expert in mind-body healing, John Diamond, M.D.[2]

Sing-Song Breath Rhythm

The best way to synchronize and harmonize breath rhythms is through singing, particularly simple songs or chants. These musical pieces are usually sung in short parallel phrases, with each phrase intoned on a single exhalation. For example, the ever-popular "Happy Birthday":

(INHALE)
Happy Birthday to you!

(INHALE)
Happy Birthday to you!

(INHALE)
Happy Birthday,
dear Mary,

(INHALE)
Happy Birthday to you!

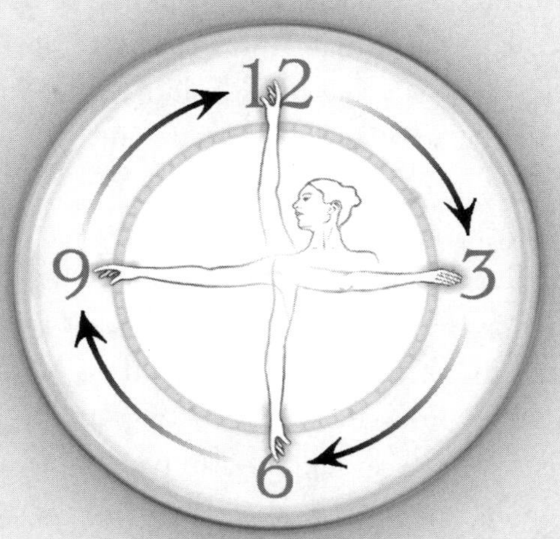

In order to find the pulse and synchronize breath rhythms while singing "Happy Birthday," stand up and use your whole arm to draw one complete circle in the space in front of you as you sing each phrase of the song. Start at six o'clock on the circle and move in a clockwise direction, ending at six o'clock when you have completed each phrase. Notice how every time you sing a phrase, your circle is absolutely the same size. This simple exercise will help you harmonize your breath rhythms, integrate your brain hemispheres, and raise your life energy, especially if you sing with devotion. Other simple yet moving tunes like "Let it Be," "Amazing Grace," and "My Country 'Tis of Thee" can also be sung while moving with the circular pulse. Lullabies connect you with this deeper pulse, too, their rhythms often literally mimicking the beating of a resting heart. As you sing, your breath capacity increases, your throat chakra opens, and you naturally receive the wisdom, guidance, and nurturance of your Essential Musical Intelligence.

Dr. Alfred A. Tomatis, a French physician and expert in psychoacoustics, tells a story about how losing one's connection with rhythmic breathing can have a deleterious effect on health and well-being. For hundreds of years, the Benedictine monks of a particular monastery in France chanted from six to eight hours a day. During the Second Vatican Council of the 1960s, an industrious new abbot decided to eliminate the chanting so that the monks could have more time for service-related activities. The monks accepted this new routine, but as the days passed, they began to feel bogged down and tired. They called a meeting to explore the cause of their fatigue. It was decided that they simply needed more sleep. Ironically, this change caused them to become even more fatigued and somewhat depressed. Doctors were called in to assess the problem. One specialist believed that the culprit was their mostly vegetarian diet, even though the monks had been eating this way for the past two hundred years. The monks added meat to their diets, but this didn't help either. When Tomatis visited the monastery, he realized that the monks had lost touch with their innate musicality (Essential Musical

Intelligence) and reintroduced chanting. Several months later, the monks were all back at work, in good health and excellent spirits.

It became obvious to Tomatis that the monks were able to work such long hours with so little sleep because of the chanting. Not only did chanting synchronize breath rhythms, which led to increased energy and vitality, but the high frequencies produced while singing literally charged the cortex of the brain, creating a kind of euphoria that allowed the monks to feel blissfully alive throughout the day and night.[3] (I will discuss this phenomenon in greater detail in chapter 6.)

Another simple, yet elegant way to synchronize breath rhythms is chanting the universal mantra, *Om* (*Aum*). According to Paramahansa Yogananda, *Aum* is the basis of all sounds. Its counterpart in the West is the word *Amen*, also known as "the Word" of the Bible. For those who have awakened the ear of the heart, it is the voice of creation testifying to the Divine Presence in every atom.[4] The mantra *Om* is actually chanted in three sections: A-U-M (AH-OH-MM), extended over one full exhalation. When your breath runs out on MM, inhale for the same length of time, sounding the *Om* silently, and continue to chant one extended A-U-M per each exhalation. Chanting *Om* for five to ten minutes each day will lead you to a place of inner peace and tranquility, allowing you to connect quite easily with your EMI.

Breath Magic and Nostril Dominance

In the lucid, quiet, anxiety-free state induced by correct diaphragmatic breathing, you will be able to explore your energy body much more easily. But first, it is important for you to become aware of natural shifts in energy reflected in the state of your nostrils. If you have been practicing the Breath Awareness exercise on a regular basis, perhaps you have noticed that one nostril is usually more open than the other at various points during the day. Shifts in nostril dominance are related to changes in hemispheric dominance of the brain.

For example, when the right nostril (associated with the *pingala* energy channel) is open, the left hemisphere is active. In this state, your consciousness is centered in a doing mentality—a linear, analytical, thinking frame of mind. When the left nostril (associated with *ida* energy channel) is open, your consciousness shifts to a right-brain mode—a receptive, emotional, creative, musical frame of mind. The primary energy channels (pingala [masculine, yang, positively charged, sun] and ida [feminine, yin, negatively charged, moon]) originate at the base of the spine and travel along either side of the sonic core that runs through the center of the spine. These channels crisscross at each chakra point along the length of the spine, creating an emotional charge at the center of each chakra that inevitably pulls us onto the various stages of the grand theater of life. The pingala and ida channels terminate at the right and left nostrils, respectively. The shifting of nostril dominance (also known as ultradian rhythms) occurs naturally every ninety minutes or so throughout the day. Usually, right around the time of the shift, both nostrils are open for a brief period. This is a highly creative state (*shushumna*) where spontaneous healing and the channeling of deeper sources of aesthetic beauty and wisdom can occur. If you can learn to recognize when you are about to enter this state, you can be more receptive to its magic.[5]

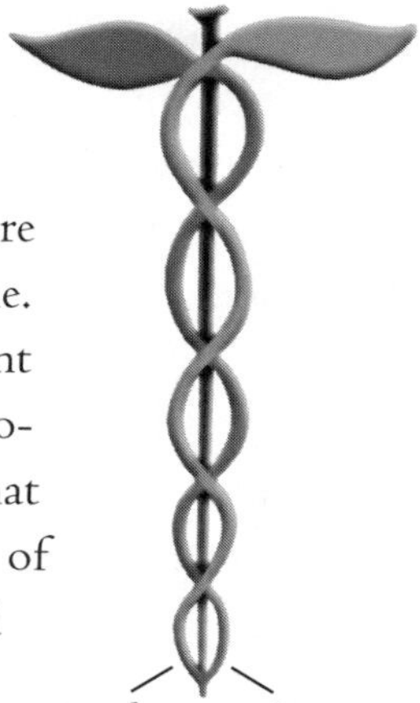

When nostril dominance becomes fixed and does not shift for long periods of time, it is an indication of impending illness. Becoming aware of blocked energy (as indicated by excessive dominance of a single nostril) before it is manifested in the physical body is an excellent form of preventive medicine. By practicing the following exercise, you will be able to purify and strengthen both energy channels so that they can work together harmoniously, leading you to a place of greater balance, harmony, order, and creative freedom.

Alternate-Nostril Breathing

Begin by sitting in an easy and steady posture with your head, neck, and trunk erect and in a straight line. Your body should be still. Bring your right hand up to your nose; your index and middle fingers should be folded so that the right thumb can be used to close your right nostril and your ring finger used to close your left nostril. With the right nostril closed, exhale completely through the left nostril. Your exhalation should be slow, controlled, and free from exertion and jerkiness. At the end of the exhalation, close your left nostril with the ring finger, open your right nostril and inhale slowly and completely. Inhalation should also be slow, smooth, controlled, and of the same duration as exhalation. Repeat this cycle two more times.

At the end of the third inhalation through your right nostril, exhale completely through the same nostril, still keeping the left nostril closed with your ring finger. At the end of this exhalation close your right nostril and inhale through the left nostril. Repeat two more times.

In summary, this exercise consists of three cycles of exhalation through the left nostril and inhalation through the right nostril, followed by three cycles of exhalation through the right nostril and inhalation through the left nostril.

Of all the self-help exercises that I have practiced over the years, alternate-nostril breathing has truly been the one that prepared me for the most positive changes in my life. It works directly with your life-force energy and its distribution through the masculine and feminine arms of consciousness. When these two forces are in balance, life becomes incredibly rhythmic, ordered, and balanced. You will no longer lapse into the grooves of laziness, doubt, indecision, or power struggles. As the polarities between your masculine and feminine energies are resolved, this spirit of harmony is projected out into the reality that you create around you. You begin to ride the wave of life instead of swimming against the current, driven by unbalanced breath rhythms and egocentric desires. (Note: To open the nostril that is blocked, lie down on the opposite side of the blocked nostril with your arm stretched out above you on the floor, your head resting in your armpit. Breathe normally for several minutes and eventually you will feel a shift. Your blocked nostril will open, allowing for clear breathing and a change in consciousness.)

APPLYING THE CONCEPT OF NOSTRIL DOMINANCE IN DAILY LIFE

Nostril open:	Active side of brain:	Recommended activities:
right	*left*	*analytical thinking, eating, and physical exercise*
left	*right*	*playing or listening to music, spiritual practice, resting, daydreaming, and contemplation*

Musical Energy Awareness

Because music is essentially vibration, it is a perfect medium for exploring the energy/breath level of consciousness. For this exercise, choose a piece of instrumental or vocal music between ten and twenty minutes long that you are not too familiar with. It could be classical, jazz, new age, or world music—the more obscure the better. Activate a state of passive volition by practicing the Breath Awareness exercise. Once you are relaxed and you have achieved the witnessing stance, lie down and let the music begin. Limit your focus to just sensing the movement of the energy of the music in and around your body. At first, you may want to focus on one particular instrument and feel where in your body its sound vibrates. You might feel it in your chest, your throat, your belly, or your hands. See if you can follow the movement of energy as you listen. Does the energy move up or down? Is it moving in or out? Does it have an integrating effect on your overall energy flow? Slowly shift your focus to other instruments and see if the energetic movement is the same or different.

Now allow yourself to focus on the rhythm of the music. Where do you feel the rhythm vibrating in your body? Allow your focus to go in and out of the physical body, becoming aware of how the music affects the energy around your body as well. Do you feel your energy body expanding or contracting as you listen? Do not be concerned with distracting thoughts that may emerge during this exercise. Simply bring your focus back to your breath, which will, in turn, allow you to connect with the music on an even deeper level than before. When the music is over, bring yourself back to ordinary consciousness and write about your experiences in your Music and Sound Awareness Journal.

Primary Energy/Breath Currents and EMI

While practicing the above exercise, you may have noticed sensations of energy coming and going in various parts of your body. There are actually five primary energy currents that work together to allow the physical body to function at optimal levels. These currents are directly affected by music and sound.

The first energy current is associated with the energy swelling upward as you inhale and is called *prāna.* Prana nourishes the mind-body and is related to the air element.

The next energy current, *apāna,* creates a sensation that courses down to the tips of your toes as you exhale to the pulse of the music. This is a cleansing energy associated with the earth element and is needed for bodily elimination.

Perhaps you experienced a gentle pulsing sensation and warmth around your solar plexus (or navel area) while listening. *Samāna,* a more subtle energy current, represents the fiery energy that facilitates digestion and is related to the need to exert or dominate.

The energy current that moves up and out is called *udāna,* and is most associated with singing and with the ether element. Udana is also related to the physiological act of vomiting.

The most subtle of the five energy currents is called *vyāna,* associated with the circulation of energy throughout the body and integration of the gestalt into a coherent system. It has been related to the development of body image and sexuality and is linked to the water element.[6,7,8]

BREATH/ENERGY CURRENTS

Name of Current	Direction of Motion	Function Served	Associated Element
Prāna	In and up	Nourishing	Air
Apāna	Down	Releasing	Earth
Samāna	Solar plexus	Igniting fire	Fire
Udāna	Up and out	Expressing	Ether
Vyāna	Integrative	Cohering	Water

Practitioners of oriental medicine, particularly the school of Ayurveda, pay special attention to the flow of the five energy currents in diagnosing and treating physical ailments. They believe that the root cause of most illnesses is disruption of the flow of one or more of these primary energy currents. Through tuning into your Essential Musical Intelligence you can become more aware while listening to different kinds of music of the flow of energy through your mind-body. With practice, you will be able to assess which currents are overstimulated or blocked. You can then choose music to bring your energy system back into balance. Working on an energy level with music and sound can help prevent physical illness.

Parts of the Prānamaya Kosha

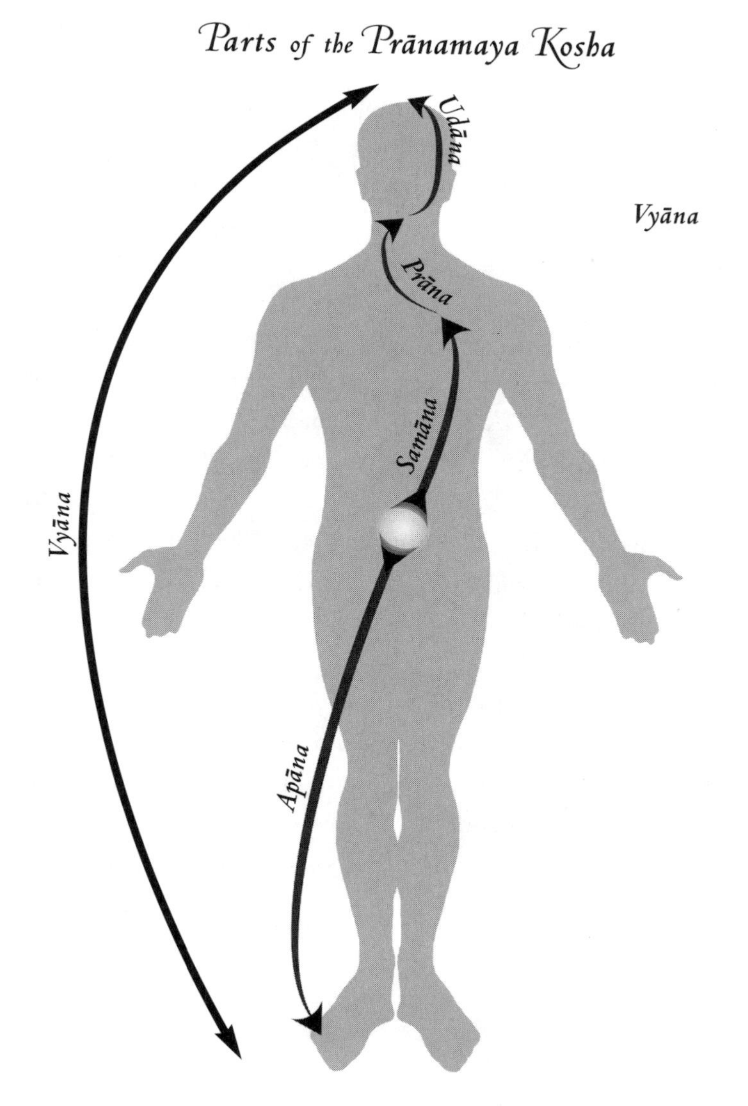

Althea, a thirty-five-year-old CEO of a graphic design company, had grappled with bulimia since leaving home for college when she was sixteen. After years of psychotherapy that she felt helped her tremendously on an emotional level, she still felt the need to binge and purge. While doing the Music Energy Awareness exercise, she realized that the udana current was overstimulated from years of vomiting. She also realized in watching her breath during the Breath Awareness exercise that she had difficulty exhaling completely. It appeared to Althea that her apana current was weak. In exploring different kinds of music, she found that moving to the beat of West African drumming allowed her breath to become deeper and to flow down to her feet. She decided to spend about thirty minutes listening and moving to the drumming for five consecutive days and then assess the affect. After her fifth music session, Althea reported that she felt like a different person: more grounded in her body, somehow safer and more secure. Although she had occasionally thought about purging during those five days, her desire to carry it out was greatly diminished. Althea continued exploring the earth-based rhythms of African music and actually joined a school where she studied African drumming and dance. When I saw her a year later, she looked radiant and told me that her bulimia was now a thing of the past.

While it is best to discover within your own music collection the pieces that seem to stimulate specific energy currents to facilitate your own health and healing, I have included Suggestions for Music Imagery (see Appendix III) based on my own research and practice that you can use to stimulate, soothe, and balance the five primary energy/breath currents.

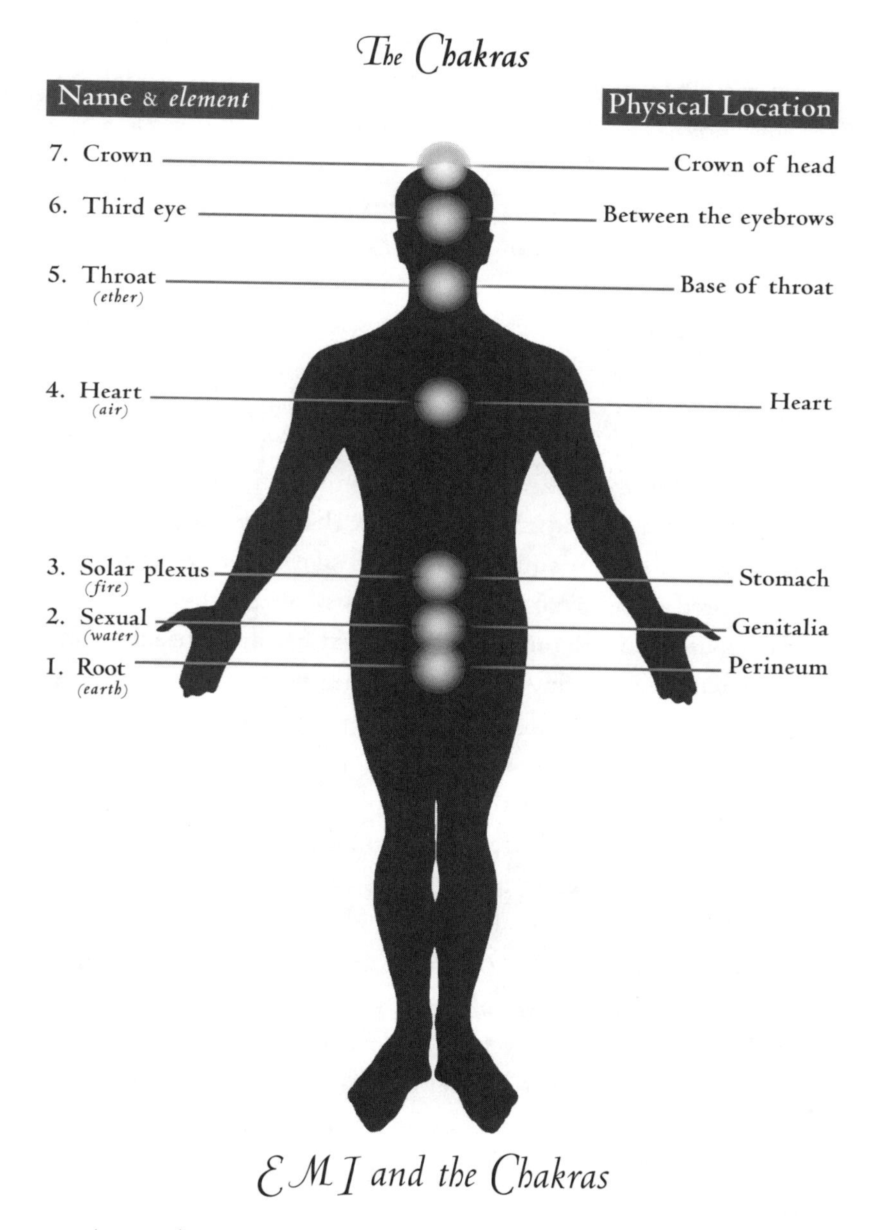

EMI and the Chakras

As you become more familiar with your energy body and how you can use music and sound to purify, strengthen, and balance the three major energy channels (ida, pingala, and shushumna) along with the five primary energy/breath currents (prana, apana, samana, udana, and vyana), it is now time to explore the seven energy vortices that color your perception of reality. From the perspective of yoga science, consciousness is expressed through the theater of the mind on seven revolving stages called *chakras.* The word *chakra* means "wheel" in Sanskrit. The chakras correspond to the important nerve plexuses located at various points along the spine.

The first chakra, at the base of the spine, is the **root (anal) chakra** (associated with the earth element and sense of smell). Above the root chakra in the region of the sacrum is the **genital chakra** (water element; taste). Next is the **solar plexus chakra** (fire element; sight), which is located slightly above the navel. These three lower chakras are associated with the animal or instinct-based side of human nature. Next come the **heart chakra** (air element; touch), and the **throat chakra** (ether element; hearing), which forms a bridge between torso and head. The sixth or **third-eye chakra**, lies between the eyebrows. The seventh center, or **crown chakra**, is at the topmost point of the skull. These four higher chakras move increasingly toward more refined, transpersonal states of consciousness.

Each chakra presents a particular drama with distinct archetypal polarities that need to be neutralized in order for you to move creatively to the next stage of evolution. In his book, *Psychotherapy East and West,* clinical psychologist Swami Ajaya describes the chakras as an integrative framework that offers us a structured inner place where we can play.[9] Through activating your Essential Musical Intelligence, you can use music and sound, the supreme vibrational healing tools to explore and resolve the polarities within this field of play, thus bringing balance and harmony to the whole self—body, mind, and spirit.

EMI as a Catalyst for Balancing Chakra Energies

You have already become familiar with the five elements (associated with the first five chakras) in chapter 2 with the Sounding the Five Elements exercise. While practicing this exercise, you probably became aware of one or more elements that seem vital and strong and perhaps others that might seem weak or blocked in some way. You may have also noticed similar effects while practicing the Musical Energy Awareness exercise. As you explore the basic polarities that exist at each chakra, you will understand how to better use music and sound to address your specific health issues.

The mode of experience at the root chakra is the struggle for survival. There are two primary polarities at this level of consciousness: predator versus prey and life versus death. The protagonist of this drama is the archetypal victim. The fight-or-flight stress reaction mentioned earlier is associated with the root chakra. If you experienced trauma during your entry into the earth plane or did not feel safe and secure growing up, you may become fixated at the level of the root chakra. In dealing with many of life's challenges then, you may typically experience yourself as a victim and consequently become hypervigilant, unable to deeply relax and just be. When centered in this level of consciousness, you may also experience emotions that you repress—destructive rage and terror. The energy required to block these powerful emotions can seriously curtail your creativity. Because many of the issues centered around the root chakra occur very early, usually before you are old enough to talk, music and sound are the most direct and efficient ways to externalize repressed feelings and bodily sensations. It is at this level that EMI can facilitate the most profound healing.

At the genital chakra, the primary issues are desire and sensory pleasure. The polarities here are pleasure versus pain and male versus female. The archetypal hedonist plays the starring role. In Western psychology, the hedonist personality is often associated with addiction. As you read in chapters 1 and 2, music can be used as a healthy substitute for an addictive substance or to transform maladaptive behavior. The second chakra is also associated with sexuality and creative drive. Music and sound can literally open up blocks to creativity, allowing you the freedom to move forward in an aesthetic flow in all areas of your life.

At the solar plexus are issues of mastery, domination, conquest, competition, inadequacy, inferiority, and pride. Here the polarities are gain versus loss, success versus failure, dominance versus submission, and blame versus praise. The archetype of the hero is most often associated with this center. The mode of experience has much to do with identity and ego development. Individuation is a keynote here as you begin in adolescence to differentiate a self separate from your parents. Many emotionally disturbed and learning-disabled children have issues at this level. Learning to play a musical instrument under the guidance of a compassionate and creative mentor or creating songs that express their unique identity and life story can help such children (and the rest of us, too) work through difficult issues that emerge at this stage of evolution.

When centered in the heart chakra, you open to compassion, generosity, selfless love, and service. The polarities presented here are that of rescuer versus rescued and liberator versus liberated. The protagonist is the archetypal mother, or savior. A great majority of people in the helping professions are centered at this level of consciousness. If you become fixated at the level of the heart chakra, however, you may neglect your own needs. This might explain the high levels of burnout in the helping professions. Listening to and playing music—alone and with others—is a wonderful mode of self-nurturing and healing when you need to recharge the batteries of the heart.

At the level of the throat chakra, you open to devotion, nurturance, unconditional love, surrender, trust, higher creativity, grace, majesty, and romance. Here the polarities are object of devotion versus devotee, mother versus child, found versus lost, and trust versus distrust. The child archetype is the main player. Many creative artists are centered in the consciousness of the throat chakra. At this stage of evolution you may begin to realize your *apparent* separation from the Divine, manifesting in a gnawing sense of abandonment and emptiness; consequently, you may feel bouts of intense sadness and longing for union, which can lead to addictions if these feelings are denied or repressed. You can explore these powerful emotions through creative musical activities such as singing, songwriting, and improvisation. When you connect with EMI at the level of the throat chakra, you can directly encounter your oneness with Absolute Being (through "musical chills" or peak experience). Once you have such an encounter, you can then transform feelings of longing and loss into the serenity and bliss of divine union.

At the third-eye center, you transcend the limitations of mind through witnessing, which allows you to open to deeper levels of insight and intuition. Thus, the third-eye chakra is the center for psychic perception. The polarities here are sage versus fool, and objective observer versus deluded participant; the lead character is the proverbial sage. When centered in this chakra, you may have the experience of channeling information from your higher self through dreams, automatic writing, artwork, poetry, and songwriting.

For example, I recently discovered an old notebook that contained several songs that I wrote in my early twenties. I had forgotten all about these songs and was curious to rediscover their inherent meaning. I was suprised at how the stories and dilemmas I had innocently conveyed through my music back then had become realities over the years. The following lyrics from a song I wrote for a young lover are particularly relevant:

> In your eyes, I see all the fortunes of dreams,
> yet you sigh and wonder,
> drift asunder,
> aimlessly at times.
> You are all you really need; life's no mystery.
> Embrace the sunlight and be as one with me.

Upon reading these word again I realized that I was actually singing to my own muse—the elusive creative self whom I was finally able to embrace much later in life. The song was a gift that, at the time, I was not yet ready to receive.

It is this sage energy that is activated when we connect with the transformational power of EMI. Although many of you have probably experienced such spontaneous wisdom, as you begin to *consciously* use EMI on a regular basis, you will expand your ability to be a clear channel for deeper truths. In time, your Essential Musical Intelligence will assist you in detaching from the limitations of the lower chakras and guide you into a consistently clear and unlimited higher reality at the level of the third eye.

No polarities exist at the level of the crown chakra. When you have resolved the polarities of the lower six chakras, you will no longer experience duality—you will finally attain unitary consciousness. You have no doubt experienced a glimmer of crown-chakra consciousness during memorable peak experiences over the course of your life. To live in this state, also known as *samadhi,* or *nirvana,* is the ultimate goal of the spiritual aspirant.

Using the Musical Five-Element Theory to Balance Chakra Energies

The following is a comprehensive system of analyzing music using the five-element theory. It was adapted from the work of musician and naturopath John Beaulieu.[10] The system draws from basic polarity principles that focus on the perpetual dance of positive and negative forces (feminine/masculine, yin/yang), the essential impetus for the development and continuation of life on this planet. As you become familiar with listening to music from this perspective, you will be able use music as a diagnostic tool in assessing the state of health or disease in each of your chakras, whether there are blocks within a particular center, whether a chakra is over- or understimulated, and if you are on the verge of breaking through to a new chakra level. If you come across blocks or imbalances in your energy centers, you can then activate your Essential Musical Intelligence in choosing appropriate music to stimulate, soothe, balance, or transform unresolved psycho-spiritual issues.

Learning to perceive the elements in music involves listening to the qualities of music (pitch, tempo, volume, and rhythm) and becoming aware of how each affects your body, mind, emotions, and spirit. It also involves trusting your intuition. You can then evaluate your responses and translate them into energetic language. Use the following system to help you choose and create music for balancing chakra energies:

Note: Since energy/breath currents are associated with the five elements, this chart could also be used to select music to balance this aspect of your energy system. However, from an energy/breath perspective, udana, whose movement is up and out in a forceful or exuberant manner, is also associated with the

	Rhytm	Tempo	Volume	Pitch
EARTH	solid, steady, forward moving	slow, controlled, stately	moderately loud	low pitched/deep - contrabass, drums, tuba, piano (African drumming)
WATER	flowing undulating, hip moving	moderately slow—medium	somewhat loud	medium low - bass clarinet, cello, bassoon, French horn, tenor sax (blues, latin jazz)
FIRE	staccato (choppy), syncopated	medium fast	loud; crescendo/decrescendo	medium high - trumpet, alto sax, English horn (flamenco, heavy metal)
AIR	swaying/swelling movements, upper body	medium to fast	medium to loud	high - violin, flute, clarinet, oboe, piccolo, alto/soprano sax (lullabies, jazz ballads)
ETHER	arrhythmic or deep breath pulse	medium to very slow	medium to soft	very high - gongs, bells, rain sticks, ocean drums (New Age Music)

element of ether. When balancing this energy/breath current, choose deeply expressive vocal music rather than the arrhythmic instrumental sound and music described here.

The best way to use the five-element system is to first assess which elements you are most drawn to in the music you are listening to right now. Is there a particular one that seems to be dominant in your listening repertoire? Do you find that there are one or more elements missing? This information provides clues as to which chakra you feel most resonant with, at which one you might be fixated, or which chakra you are resisting because of unresolved issues.

For example, Marge, a Generation X neighbor, listens to music constantly. I don't think I've even seen her without her headphones. When I asked what she spends so much time listening to, she explained that she vacillates between Charlie Parker and Miles Davis (especially songs played at fast tempos), heavy metal, and ambient club music. She likes the buzz she feels while listening to fast music. She also likes turning up the volume on her Discman, especially while walking around the city. She says it is invigorating. She hates music with a funky beat or anything by the Gipsy Kings.

Using the musical five-element theory, I could gain a bit of insight into Marge's chakra energies. What stands out immediately is her love of fast tempos. This falls into the category of the air element. She also likes loud music. This too falls into the air category. She listens a lot to Charlie Parker (alto sax; fire element) and Miles Davis (trumpet; fire element). Most heavy-metal music fits into the fire category; ambient club music, the air element again. So Marge is heavily loaded on fire and air, which are associated with the solar plexus and heart chakras, respectively. She hates funky music and the Gipsy Kings. Both kinds of music tend to fall into the water and earth (hip-moving, sensual, passionate) categories.

In getting to know Marge better over the last few months, I have discovered that she has chronic colitis (associated with earth-chakra imbalance) and suffers from terrible PMS every month (water-chakra issues). This information actually confirmed Paracelsus' aphorism, "As in life, so in music." Perhaps in limiting her exposure to certain types of music, Marge is running away (air and fire chakras) from emotional or energetic blocks related to her earth and water chakras.

To harmonize the chakra imbalances reflected in both Marge's choice of music and her physical disorders, I might suggest to Marge that she practice Sounding the Five Elements as a warm-up to help her feel comfortable using sound to explore the elemental energy of each chakra. When she begins to warm up to her earth and water centers, along with the archetypal energies of her throat chakra, I might then introduce varying types of music that contain the disowned elements, starting with etheric music, moving gradually to water music, and then music with a strong earth component. I would remember, of course, to use the iso principle to respect Marge's own innate musical choices and avoid shocking her with music that is foreign or distasteful to her musical palate. Opening up to the archetypal energies of her neglected chakras might actually help to release blocked emotions associated with Marge's physical problems.

Now it is your turn. In your Music and Sound Awareness Journal, make a list of the five pieces of music that you are particularly drawn to at the present time. Analyze the music using the five-element theory and assess your overall chakra strengths, weaknesses, and levels of integration. If there is a particular center that you would like to focus on, tune into your EMI and allow it to direct you to the music that will facilitate greater awareness, clarity, and transformation. Record in your journal any important insights and physiological and/or emotional changes you experience. Don't forget to include music that repels you or that you find yourself resisting, since this reaction may indicate an emotional blockage—most likely an aversion to an unacceptable aspect of yourself associated with a particular chakra level. In a safe and supportive environment, explore the feelings that are triggered by the music. You might be surprised at what you find. (For a list of musical selections organized according to their dominant elements, see Appendix V.)

In the following chapters, you will learn many more musical techniques for understanding the dynamics of each chakra and how you can use your EMI to balance, harmonize, and strengthen chakra energies for perfect health, harmonious relationships, and greater abundance.

Chapter Four

Music as Mind: Witnessing

The existence of illness in the body may be called a shadow of the true illness [which] is held by man in his mind. By the power of music the mind may become exalted so that it rises above the thought of illness; then the illness is forgotten.

—Hazrat Inayat Khan

Through utilizing your Essential Musical Intelligence, you have now learned to turn inward to observe the more subtle energy/breath plane and how it interacts with the physical body. You have also honed your ability to relax and balance your chakra energies with music and sound. These activities bring you to a point of stillness where you can then begin to observe the realm of mind. The mind is even more subtle than the energy/breath level and infinitely more powerful. It consists of your thoughts, feelings, memories, attitudes, beliefs, wishes, fantasies, and desires. Through its multitude of functions, the mind allows you to construct your own template of reality and to manifest your unique identity within it. In essence, your mind is the vehicle through which you create your world. As you become more aware of its idiosyncratic rhymes and reasons through your deepening relationship with EMI, you will be able to gradually transcend its limitations and create harmony, balance, and beauty in every dimension of your life.

In bringing together both Eastern and Western perspectives on the purpose, function, and organization of the mental body, it appears that what we know as "mind" can be understood by exploring its four distinct yet interactive components:

1. **The sensory-motor mind** receives sense impressions and coordinates them with motor responses.
2. **The ego** organizes sense impressions from the perspective of "I."
3. **The discriminative faculty** helps you make decisions.
4. **The subconscious mind** is the storehouse of memories, experiences, and impressions, and contains both your personal unconscious (forgotten and/or repressed memories), and what Swiss psychoanalyst Carl Jung called the "collective unconscious," or the innate psychological activity that transcends personal experience and relates directly to the archetypal and instinctual bases of human life (the hero, witch, and so on).[1]

At an even subtler level, the subconscious also houses what psychoanalyst Christopher Bollas calls the "unthought known," the body-based, cellular memory of the emotional climate of the early home environment that we all internalize as "inner music."[2] This inner music is experienced as an almost imperceptible yet pervasive mood (hunger, melancholy, anxiety) woven indelibly into the fabric of consciousness. Until it is actually "heard," externalized, and examined, the feeling tone of your inner music subtly colors your self-concept and perception of reality throughout your lifetime, without your conscious control.

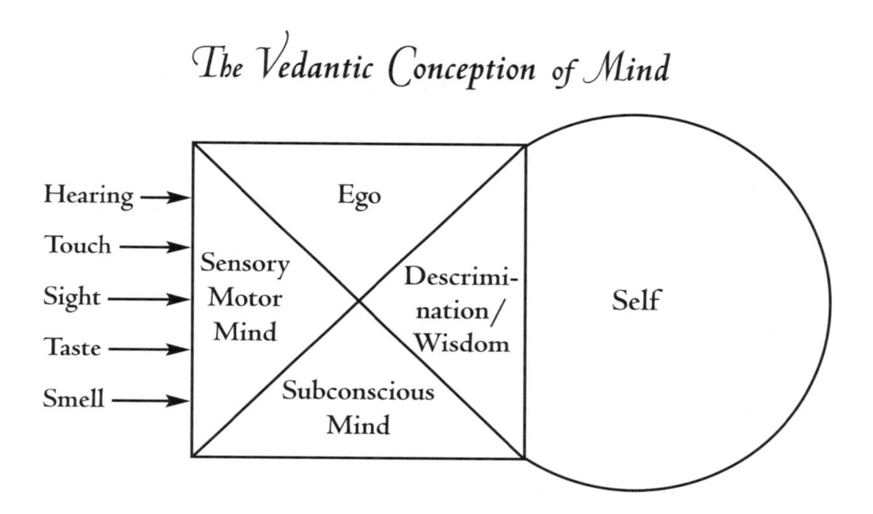

Many people are not aware of the different levels and functions of the mind and their powerful effect on mental and physical health and healing. To become aware, you must be willing to turn inward and systematically observe your thoughts, feelings, desires, perceptions, beliefs, and attitudes. Your Essential Musical Intelligence provides a safe and supportive holding environment for such exploration. As you will see, music mirrors the various dimensions of mind. In a playful, nonthreatening way, music can guide you in creatively navigating and transforming this vast internal landscape.

Common issues at the level of mind run the gamut from benign everyday kinds of fears and anxieties like, "Will I get my paycheck today?" to devastating addictions, psychosomatic illnesses, and suicidal or homicidal tendencies. The root cause of most psychological problems can be traced to early unresolved developmental issues that correspond to the natural unfolding of the energies of the first three chakras.

For example, at the root chakra, you deal with issues of safety and security. Conflicts at this level evoke primitive feelings of fear, terror, anger, and rage. At the second chakra, attachment is key, along with issues surrounding pleasure versus pain. Imbalances here are often related to addiction and codependence. At the third chakra, you address problems of power and control, which often manifest as identity issues. With more serious mental disturbances, there are imbalances at all three chakra levels.

When there is early trauma (loss, abuse, overwhelming physical and emotional pain), the evolving ego is not strong enough to handle the intensity of the experience. In order to cope with the chaos and confusion, it literally fragments into separate ego states. Often, one or more of these ego states are frozen in time and forgotten. This process is called "dissociation." As a result, some parts of the ego develop normally while other parts remain traumatized or fixated at the original age the trauma occurred. For most people, dissociative tendencies are unconscious and can hinder one's sincere efforts toward psychological and spiritual growth. Trauma-related dissociation has also been linked to many psychosomatic illnesses. We will discuss using EMI to deal with fragmentation of the ego in chapter 8.

Inevitably, somewhere along the line of self-development we get stuck and our mental health is compromised in one way or another. This stuckness is manifested not only in our thoughts and feelings, but also in our behaviors, attitudes and beliefs, family, social, and professional relationships, and in our bodies. You can use EMI to facilitate healing on the level of the mind in two fundamental ways: the first is to strengthen and expand your identity (ego) by shining light into the dark, painful places of the unknown mind, thereby making the unconscious known. This is related to the first phase of activating EMI—the *witnessing stance* associated with self-observation and inner listening.

The second way is to develop your discriminative function, which allows you to choose the most efficient ways of thinking and feeling and supports your ability to manifest your highest good throughout your lifetime. It also represents the second phase of EMI activation—*transformation*. When you call upon your EMI to create harmony in the face of dissonant thoughts and feelings, you hasten your healing process immeasurably.

Most of your mental functioning is based on habits of thought, feeling, and behavior that are molded into your basic identity structure. These habits have allowed you to function in the world with varying degrees of success. Like grooves in a record, these mental activities repeat endlessly without your conscious awareness. Some habits are adaptive, while others can be deleterious to your health. Generally speaking, the development of habits is based on the pleasure principle: we embrace the thoughts, feelings, and behaviors that bring pleasure and shy away from those that provoke fear or pain.

After his fiancée left him about a year ago, Russell was devastated. For months he complained regularly to his friends and coworkers about his loneliness and fear that he would never find a suitable partner. When friends invited him to events where he could meet available women, his fear of rejection strongly outweighed his spirit of adventure, and he repeatedly declined. Instead he habitually spent Saturday nights at home alone watching *Seinfeld* reruns and eating a pint of Häagen Dazs chocolate ice cream, feeling safe but sorry.

Russell is not at the mercy of his habitual thoughts and feelings, however—and neither are you. Maladaptive habits can be transformed by observing your thoughts and behaviors, evaluating them, and making a conscious decision to change. The transformational aspect of EMI can wonderfully assist you. Its presence will continually remind you of your ability to transcend limitations by tuning into the creative essence of your being—the aspect of self that is open to growth and change—and to physically manifest your highest good through heartfelt musical expression. Through connecting with EMI, you can live fully in the creative moment, surrendering to the intuitive voice of your core self, unhampered by the ego or instinct-driven habits.

Jennifer is a gifted painter who has supported herself through her art for a number of years. While she knew that having her own web page could make her work more accessible to the public, she felt overwhelmed at the thought of working with computers. She decided to use her Essential Musical Intelligence to understand her ambivalence toward technology. After practicing the first of the Six Steps to Healing and identifying her problem—terror at the thought of learning how to set up her own web page—Jennifer practiced the Breath Awareness exercise to center herself. Then she focused on step 2, remembering her true worth. She reminded herself that her success in life truly mattered and that she deserved to be loved and supported . She then called upon her EMI for help (step 3). She breathed into her throat chakra, imagined the whole area filling up with light, and opened herself to receiving inspiration and guidance (step 4). As she contemplated her problem, a memory suddenly emerged: she had been severely criticized by her third-grade math teacher. Jennifer remembered feeling terribly humiliated and incompetent. From that point on, she had been afraid to learn anything that involved complex numerical procedures.

The next step for Jennifer (step 5) was to take action—to express herself through a musical activity that could transform her feelings of incompetence. She began to tone a low-pitched OH sound into her solar plexus. After stoking her creative fire with the OH sound for several minutes, she spontaneously created a musical affirmation, "I trust in my ability to think logically and sequentially. I am competent and powerful as can be." She began to sing her new affirmation throughout the day. A wave of comfort and positive expectation flowed through her for which she was deeply grateful (step 6). A couple of days later Jennifer saw an advertisement for a course in web-page design and, humming her affirmation, she called to register. Jennifer used her affirmation throughout the entire learning process, and her web page ultimately brought her greater success in her business. She also gained more confidence to confront other areas of her life where she experienced fear and limitation.

Witnessing

An excellent way to gain control over the modifications of the mind is through witnessing. Witnessing is an attribute of the next level of consciousness, the intellect/intuition realm. It is your ability to simply observe with detachment the ever-changing stream of thoughts, feelings, beliefs, perceptions, and attitudes that continually flows through your mind. As thoughts arise, you note them and gently return your focus to the task at hand.

You can develop the witnessing stance through focusing activities such as meditation, hatha yoga, martial arts, and contemplative activities involving the creative arts, enjoyment of nature, and prayer. As the witnessing part of you gets better at focusing, the "monkey of your mind" grows tired of being ignored and eventually quiets down. Then you can arrive at a state of uninterrupted peace and tranquility where you can finally rest and just be.

While traditional meditation techniques can be helpful in reconnecting you with your Essential Musical Intelligence, the following music-meditation exercise might be even more beneficial. Listening to music is a natural way to develop concentration. The spirit in the music captivates your attention and pulls you along to its destination. The sensual, emotionally evocative quality of certain kinds of music brings the decidedly mental practice of concentration to a feeling level, thus integrating head and heart. It is at this point of integration that the potential for deep healing lies. Another benefit of focusing with music (particularly sacred music) is its natural capacity to lead us into states of peace and stillness. Devotional music also has the added function of awakening spiritual longing, joy, awe, and unconditional love. The most profound benefit of music meditation, however, takes place in the silence after the music has ended. In this place of quiet solitude, we connect with the essential self, our true identity.

Music Meditation

The mind cannot observe itself. Who then is observing?

Begin by choosing a selection of music between twenty and thirty minutes in length that is calm, serene, and devotional. Look for music that has long, synchronous breath rhythms with which you can entrain. This will help slow your heart rhythms and connect you with your EMI. Music with a combination of the elements ether and water works quite well. Some examples might be Gregorian chant, Japanese shakuhachi flute, meditative solo piano (George Winston), or traditional Indian ragas (Gandharva Veda music). Before turning on the music, practice diaphragmatic breathing to ground and center yourself. Next, do three rounds of alternate-nostril breathing to harmonize and balance your life energy.

Now you are ready to begin your music meditation. Turn on your recording. Sit in an upright position with head, neck, and trunk aligned and continue breathing diaphragmatically as you follow the movement of the music. Try these two listening techniques: bring your awareness to the outer rims of your ears and feel the music expand your listening and take you where you need to go. Next, focus on the pulse of the music as it resonates in your heart center. You might even be able to feel the beating of your heart as you breathe in and out through your heart chakra along with the pulse of the music. Choose your favorite of the two techniques and stay with it for the duration of the exercise. If distracting thoughts or feelings emerge, do not give them any energy. Gently bring your focus back to the music. When the music is over, rest in the quiet stillness of the moment and allow it to expand for as long as you are comfortable. You may end your meditation with an affirmation for healing, abundance, or anything that brings greater peace and joy into your life and the lives of all sentient beings.

By practicing this music meditation regularly, you strengthen your ability to focus inward and connect with the more hidden aspects of mind where most psychological problems originate. It also strengthens your capacity to truly *be with* troubling thoughts and emotions in a dispassionate way, rather than engaging in defensive maneuvers to keep them hidden. You may want to use the same music each time you practice or experiment with different kinds of music to evoke a variety of thoughts and feelings. The most important thing is to do the music meditation regularly and use your Music and Sound Awareness Journal to chart your progress. With time, you will increase your ability to concentrate, remain calm and centered amidst chaotic thoughts and feelings, reach deeper levels of peace and stillness, and release your ego identifications in order to merge with your deeper self.

EMI and Emotions

While learning to detach from the controlling influence of your thoughts can help you to be more present and focused in the here-and-now, it is even more important to understand the source of your emotions and how they affect health and healing. In essence, emotions that emanate from the four primary instinctual urges—self-preservation, sleep, food, and sex—are much more powerful than thoughts. Clinical research indicates that emotional memories can distort our perceptions and override conscious thought.[4] This explains why trying to change maladaptive thoughts with positive thinking doesn't always work. It is now quite evident that it takes a power stronger than the mind to change deep emotional patterning. This is where EMI comes in. EMI operates from a level beyond the mind. Through engaging your Essential Musical Intelligence, the coherent power and intelligence of the heart and third-eye chakras, and communicative capacity of the throat chakra are activated to facilitate deep and lasting transformation on the emotional plane.

From a mind-body perspective, emotions are innate psychobiological signals that provide information for the aware individual. They provide us with data about our physical, existential, spiritual, psychological, and social states of being. According to current psychoneuroimmunological research, the old system of labeling emotions as either positive or negative no longer holds water. Instead, a new model of the emotions—the spectrum model—asserts that all emotions are innately neutral and that mind-body healing utilizes the full spectrum.[5] Through your engagement with music, you can naturally experience and integrate the complete range of emotions. These experiences can help you create a more cohesive sense of self, resulting in increased coherence in your bodily processes and within your social environment.

From the perspective of health and healing, research indicates that expressing emotionally relevant issues lowers sympathetic nervous system activity, improves immunity, and reduces the likelihood of disease. For people in the grip of serious illness, open emotional expression and group support significantly impact mortality, disease remission, and immune function. Over a dozen writing studies and several music therapy studies document beneficial health and other effects associated with meaningful self-disclosure.[6,7,8] It is obvious that engaging music to explore the emotions, along with verbal processing (journaling), can be quite salutary to your overall mental and physical health.

Music and Mother

The connection between music and feelings can be traced back to our earliest relationship with Mother.[9] Even in the womb, the fetus picks up all the vibrational emanations of the mother—her bodily rhythms, acute emotions, fluctuating moods and cravings, and most importantly, her thoughts and orientation toward the unborn child. The developing fetus bonds with the rhythm of the mother's heartbeat, its source of life. The regular rhythm of Mother's heart creates a state of homeostasis during intrauterine life. A number of psychoanalytic writers agree that our deep fascination with music has its roots in the sound contact between mother and fetus. One analyst writes, "Music is the evocation of mother; [its purpose] is to reedit the relationship with her and with nature."[10]

In taking the music-mother connection a bit further, it is interesting to note that mothers intuitively communicate with their babies through music. This style of communication is called "Motherese."[11] Motherese is defined as the unique pattern of sounds that caregivers the world over use to communicate with infants. Stanford psychologist Anne Fernald, in her research with European and Asian mothers and babies, found dramatic differences between the way mothers talk to adults and the way they talk to babies. When talking to adults, mothers use a lower frequency tone and speak more quickly, with shorter pauses. Universal melodies seem to emerge during mother-child interactions. This melodic speech is almost always communicated at a significantly higher pitch level. The research shows that babies seem to prefer the Motherese style of communication regardless of the actual language.

It is my contention that babies, because they have not yet developed any defenses or judgments to mask their innocence, instantly awaken our Essential Musical Intelligence. They are pure expressions of love, and we naturally respond to them in this way.

Lullabies

Another universal musical phenomenon in mother-child interaction is the lullaby. In every culture there exist simple songs to lull babies to sleep. These songs are traditionally passed on orally from generation to generation. Lullabies are typically composed in a gentle rocking waltzlike rhythm (three-quarter time) and most often have melodies made up of triadic intervals. The rocking rhythms and simple melodies create a sense of predictability and safety for the vulnerable newborn and mother. Lullabies also provide a bridge for rhythmic bonding between the mother and child during intrauterine life. The lullaby is a song of the heart that reflects the rhythm of the mother's heartbeat, along with her deep love and desire to nurture her newborn treasure.

Recently, one of my students recounted an old Jewish folk tale that suggests the origin of the word *lullaby.* The story revolves around the transformation of Lilith, the first woman created by God, from goddess to demon when she was unfairly expelled from the Garden of Eden because of her unwillingness to be subservient to Adam. Lilith became outraged and bitter, and in an act of revenge, threatened to destroy any newborn who crossed her path. The story goes on to say that mothers would sing the *Lilith-by* to protect their infants from her terrible wrath.

Along these same lines, you too can use the lullaby as a healing force in your own life. Occasionally, when we are in situations where we are about to give birth to some creative project that we truly value, we come face-to-face with imaginary demons (also known as inner critics) who threaten to wreak havoc in our lives. These inner critics, the internalized negative judgmental voices of significant others, endeavor to sabotage our good feelings about ourselves and take the joy out of our creative pursuits. It is here that you can use the lullaby as an EMI tool to create an aura of safety when you feel attacked by inner critics or whenever you need comfort.

Create Your Own Lullaby

Which lullabies do you remember from your childhood? If you cannot recall one, do not fret. You will now create a lullaby of your own that you can use to soothe and nurture the musical child within. You might want to have your Music and Sound Awareness Journal and tape recorder nearby to record the creative insights that come to you during this exercise. Begin by accessing an image of yourself rocking a tiny infant in your arms. Let all of your senses engage with this image. Feel the soft, grainy texture of the cotton baby blanket next to your skin. Smell the clean, pure scent of your innocent little baby. Feel the waves of your heartbeat as you rock your baby in sync with the universal pulse. Feel the vibration of unconditional love as it wells up from the heart to your throat and then out through your loving voice and arms. When you feel ready, listen for the words to your lullaby. They may come to you in a stream of consciousness or as a rhyme. You might want to work with rhythm first. Use a rain stick, Tibetan bell bowl, ocean drum, or shaker to create a soothing rhythm. Take all the time you need. You will know when you are finished, as the music will feel effortless and natural to perform. If you play an instrument, you might want to accompany yourself or play a solo section after you have sung the first verse or two.

The lullaby is a wonderful way to nurture your inner child. It is this very real part of us that experiences intense anxiety stemming from early unresolved abandonment issues and feels the depths of depression and despair when its nurturing object is missing. Singing your own special lullaby at such times can recreate (or create for the first time) the experience of being loved and held by an ideal mother.

Clarisse had a high-powered job as executive director of a thriving mental-health agency in New York City. Upon first meeting her, you would think that Clarisse had it all—a fulfilling career, successful marriage, beautiful home, and more money than she knew what to do with. However, she was plagued with low-grade depression, a gnawing feeling that at the core of her being she was flawed and thus unlovable. She told me that when she was two years old, her mother sent her to live with a childless friend of the family who soon adopted her and became her new mother. Clarisse's birth mother then went on to have ten more children, most of whom she kept.

Although Clarisse described her childhood with her adoptive mother as relatively happy, she always felt separate from others and a bit lonely. She was haunted by the issue of why and how her birth mother could have given her away. This mystery caused her tremendous pain. I suggested that Clarisse activate her EMI and write a lullaby for the two-year-old who felt so confused and abandoned. I told Clarisse that she might never be able to come to terms with her birth mother's actions, but that she could become a loving and nurturing mother to her own inner child. Amidst much resistance, anger, and tears, Clarisse wrote the following lullaby:

Reunion

When you are feeling so sad and alone,
I'll scoop you up, baby, and bring you back home—
Home to a garden where you've never been,
Filled with sweet fruits and your closest of kin.

For years I've been waiting for you to arrive,
For when you are near me, I feel so alive.
You're precious sweet darling, don't ever forget.
I'm with you forever, so have no regret.

Through contacting her EMI and creating the lullaby, Clarisse was able to become her own ideal mother and musically embrace the part of her that felt discarded and unworthy of love. She found within her own heart the ability to acknowledge the preciousness of her inner child and to realize that she was not necessarily like her birth mother, that she (Clarisse) would do anything for this child, who was special and infinitely worthy and that she would never again abandon her own self. Clarisse sang this lullaby as part of a daily healing ritual over a period of several weeks. She then continued to sing the song whenever she felt plagued with feelings of emptiness and despair. Gradually, over time, the new feelings engendered by the lullaby were woven into the fabric of her consciousness and her "inner music" began to sound a different tune.

The Musical Mind

Although it is quite fascinating that we use music to communicate with and nurture the developing neonate, it is even more remarkable that, according to cutting-edge research in early infant development, the essential fabric of our cognitive and emotional lives *is* music. In his book, *Diary of a Baby,* noted developmental psychologist Daniel Stern describes in refreshingly musical terms how three-month-old Joey perceives having just turned away from the sunlit wall of his room to look at the bars of his crib, and to then gaze past them to the darker far wall:

Suddenly a piece of space stands out.
It's a pillar, thin and taut.
It stands motionless and sings out a bright melody.
Now, from close by, different notes drift in.
There is nearby another pillar of space.
It, too, sings—but in harmony with the first.
The two melodies mingle in a tight duet,
one melody loud, the other quiet.
Far away, large, soft volumes now show themselves.
They beat out a slower, deeper rhythm.
The near, bright duet runs in and out of the far,
    slow rhythm.
The two spaces weave together into a single song that
    fills the world.
Then, from somewhere else, sounds a different note.
A shooting star, it flashes past and quickly disappears.[12]

After twenty years of conducting intensive research on early infant development, Stern, along with several of his colleagues, concludes that the human infant's earliest experience of life is a musical one. According to Stern, every object and person with whom the infant comes in contact expresses a particular feeling tone. These feeling tones are incorporated into the infant's perceptual schema. As the infant interacts more and more with his environment, the accumulated feeling tones or inner music take on a life of their own, forming a rudimentary framework for emotional interaction and communication.[13]

In studying the early infant-mother relationship, Stern also discovered a musical foundation. Stern believes that the relationship between mother and baby is made of temporal structures that permit emotional experiences to be represented. It is interesting to note, incidentally, that *music* is made of temporal structures that permit emotional experiences to be represented.

For example, because the infant cannot yet understand language, the mother, in a singsong way (Motherese), engages the baby in a kind of rhythmical call and response. Mommy makes a loving musical statement and waits for a response from baby; baby's eyes widen and she responds with a smile, gurgle, and coo; Mother mirrors the baby's response (in rhythm) and then elaborates on her original musical statement.

Such communication takes place within specific temporal structures that seem to be innately rooted in the expressive capacity of both mother and baby. This spontaneous call and response can be likened to what is called "trading fours" in jazz improvisation. An exquisite example can be heard on a live recording of Ella Fitzgerald and Louis Armstrong (Satchmo) trading fours on the Ellington-Mills tune, "It Don't Mean a Thing If It Ain't Got That Swing" (from the Verve album, *First Lady of Song*). After she sings the tune through once, Ella playfully scats over a chorus. Then she and Satchmo trade fours for a chorus. First Ella scats a phrase over four bars of the song, then Satchmo scats back, complementing her phrase with his own dynamic musicality within the same temporal frame. They go on like that for an entire chorus. The music builds to a frenzied intensity and the listeners go wild. Could it be that this improvisational call-and-response aspect of jazz is actually touching upon the listeners' cellular memory of their first intimate communications with Mother?

Within these temporal structures are what Stern calls vitality affects, properties of feelings (as well as of music) that represent the underlying, nonreferential dynamic elements associated with specific emotional states. For example, the vitality affect of tightness can be associated with feeling angry, sad, frustrated, or pleased. Vitality affects involve properties of shape, contour, intensity, motion, number, and rhythm, and may be expressed through any of the senses. These basic expressive (musical) qualities are a far more accurate gauge of how we feel than the words we speak.

For example, fear can have a number of vitality affects: constriction (diminution of life energy); shaking (tremolo); stiff and arrhythmical movements of the body; raised pitch and decreased volume of the speaking voice (due to stifled breathing). With anger, we experience the vitality affects of tightness, staccato movements, shakiness (tremolo), and increased volume and pitch of the speaking voice. With love, there are significant differences. The vitality affects are those of smoothness; harmony; gentleness of gesture; a soft, full tone in the speaking voice; and in jazz lingo, a sense of "swing" and "tastiness." All of the above vitality affects are deeply encoded in the inner musical memories of our first years of life. They are spontaneously activated when we listen to music; hence, the music-mother-emotion connection. From a more scientific perspective, it is also fascinating to note that music naturally bypasses the cortical functioning or thinking part of the brain and moves directly to the limbic system (emotional brain center). This again suggests that the origins of mental functioning and emotional intelligence are rooted in music.

Vitality Affects

Emotion	**Musical Qualities**
fear	constriction (minor intervals); shaking (tremolo); arrhythmical; raised pitch and decrescendo (decrease in volume)
anger	tightness (minor intervals); staccato; shakiness (tremolo); crescendo (pitch rises dramatically) and forte (increase in volume)
love	smoothness (major intervals); harmonic; flowing; sense of swing

So how does all of this relate to health and healing of the mental body? During the first year or so of life, the infant does not yet have the cognitive capacity to make sense of emotional interactions with caregivers. It records the presymbolic, felt sense of these experiences in procedural memory. Our earliest experience of life then is encoded in a body-based cellular memory in the form of inner music, which becomes a mostly inaudible backdrop of consciousness that accompanies us as we develop through life. These memories cannot be retrieved through the thinking mind. They speak to us through the body in the form of physical sensations and/or symptoms and through our reactions to music, both while we listen and play. The music of our early emotional lives is also reflected in the dynamics of our interpersonal relationships and in our recurring moods and fantasies. These musical memories, left unexplored and unconscious, are often the root cause of psychological problems and psychosomatic illnesses. It is here where your EMI can be of immeasurable value in facilitating healing.

How can you reconnect with this early felt sense—your cellular musical memory? Within the context of EMI, music becomes a self-reflecting and transformational tool in facilitating self-awareness and unearthing and healing any dissonance embedded in the unthought known (inner music). There are two primary modalities that you can use to help you in becoming more aware of your inner music: intentional music listening and creative musical expression, especially improvisation. We begin with the following music-listening exercise.

Music and Mind Awareness

Choose a piece of instrumental music, preferably classical, that lasts for twenty to thirty minutes, such as the first movement of Gorecki's Symphony No. 3, Op. 36. Exclude anything that you have analyzed musically or that carries strong emotional associations. As in the other listening exercises, find a time and space where you will not be disturbed. You may want to recline and close your eyes so that you can sink into your own internal world. As you breath deeply and rhythmically, let go of tension and worry and allow yourself to become completely immersed in the music. As you listen, be aware of how you process the music. Do you experience imagery? Is the music telling a story? Do you feel bodily sensations, such as involuntary movements, increased heart rate, changes in skin temperature? Perhaps the music brings up memories from a time in your life when you heard it before. Some people have peak experiences while listening and become one with the music in a kind of spiritual reverie. Whatever happens, be sure to allow yourself time to process your specific reactions to the music after you have completed the exercise.

You may have a number of different reactions to the Music and Mind Awareness exercise. For most people, listening to music in a focused, relaxed state stimulates the imagination. According to recent neuropyschological research, there is a strong connection in the brain between the centers for auditory processing and image formation. Many of the images stimulated by music are archetypal in nature and evoke specific emotions in groups of listeners.

For example, I often used different types of classical music to stimulate imagery during weekly therapy sessions with a group of emotionally disturbed preadolescent boys. For the first couple of months, every piece that I played evoked images of violence and destruction (expressed through their drawings), along with feelings of fear, tension, and anger. One piece had a dramatically different effect—a mass by fourteenth-century cleric and poet Guillerme Machaut. After listening to this music in a relaxed state, most of the boys drew images of churches, crosses, or lovely nature scenes. (Note: The boys were not told the name of the piece until after they had completed their drawings.) The most disturbed boy in the group drew a radiant rainbow and wrote under the arc, "I love this music." I was quite surprised, but thought that perhaps the boys' reaction was just a reflection of their having a particularly good day, or that they were now feeling safe enough to express more vulnerable feelings. But there was something about that particular piece . . . It seems that every time I use Machaut's Mass as the focus of the Music and Mind Awareness exercise, listeners have similar reactions. Obviously, this music awakens deeply held archetypal memories and feelings that can lead to transformation if and when the listener is ready.

While practicing the Music and Mind Awareness exercise, you may find strong personal associations to certain pieces of music. The vitality affects inherent in a particular work can transport you back to the moment in your life when you experienced a specific quality of emotion. For example, the first movement of Beethoven's Pastoral Symphony might activate memories of joyful moments spent in nature when you were a small child. Bach's Passacaglia and Fugue in C Minor, which has vitality affects that express qualities of sadness and loss, might evoke actual memories and feelings about the loss of a significant other. Each of these musical memories can release emotional energies that fuel the creative fires within and facilitate wholeness.

Tuning into the personal and collective unconscious through the Music and Mind Awareness exercise can take you where you need to go in your own artistic exploration and growth. You may experience synesthesia, a phenomenon in which music evokes brilliant changing colors that inspire the painter within. Music can also arouse the dancer in you. One of my students, Jamie, a professional dancer and choreographer, listened to the Gorecki composition and envisioned the beginning of a dance piece. She saw two circles of women dressed in black. One circle moved slowly and steadily in a clockwise direction, and the other circle moved in the opposite direction in a fast-paced chaotic fashion. Jamie was able to use this highly charged musical image, which reflected some important unresolved personal issues, in choreographing a dance for her company's next performance.

You may also have strong emotional reactions to the music. As philosopher Suzanne Langer wrote, music sounds the way feelings feel.[14] The feeling tone of a particular work can unlock hidden emotions that carry a similar feeling tone. You may rise to heights of joy and ecstasy or be moved to tears, but as T. S. Eliot realized, "You are the music while the music lasts." Feelings pass, and when the music is over, you will return to center. If in some way you feel adversely affected while practicing this exercise, open your eyes, come back to ordinary reality, turn the music off, and ground yourself through breathing, toning, journaling, or contacting a close friend or therapist.

Finally, you might enjoy peak experiences while communing with the music. Several students who practiced this exercise were able to merge with their Essential Musical Intelligence and achieve a transcendent feeling of oneness with all life while listening. A few have even experienced spontaneous healing in this spiritually awakened state. (Scientific research indicates that the thrills associated with a musical peak experience are related to the release of endorphins, our body's natural painkillers.[15]) Again, the point of this listening exercise is to become more aware of your inner music at various levels of the mind. It is important to record what you have learned from this exercise in your Music and Sound Awareness Journal. Writing helps to ground significant memories and insights that emerge from your musical journeys so that you can explore them in depth at a later time. Your inner life is important. The more time you allot to your communion with your inner music, the more energy is available for creativity, and the more prepared you are to share your creative gifts with humanity.

EMI, Mind, and Playing

You are now ready to move from listening to recorded music to playing music. Renowned psychoanalyst Donald Winnicott writes that it is only in playing that the child (and adult) is free to be creative, *and it is only in being creative that the individual discovers the self.*[16] In his book, *Playing and Reality,* Winnicott writes about the need for the young child to differentiate a self separate from its mother. According to Winnicott, up until age two, the infant experiences himself as the center of existence. During this phase his emotions are intense and polarized. He experiences Mother as either all good or all bad, depending upon whether or not his needs are met. As the infant matures, he begins to realize that Mother is a whole person with a life of her own who will not always be there to take care of his every need. This realization leads to a depressive period in which the child mourns the loss of the ideal mother.

Around the same time, the infant begins the process of separation and individuation. He chooses a transitional object, a cherished possession that he can substitute for Mother that can be affectionately cuddled and loved as well as mutilated. The transitional object (blanket or teddy bear) must never change unless changed by the infant and must survive instinctual love, hate, and pure aggression. In order to test the limits of his relationship with his transitional object and move into his unique identity and relationship to the real world, the infant needs a field of play where the emotional dynamics of relationships with objects can be examined, experienced in symbol, thought about, and processed. In this transitional space, the child can be both omnipotently creative (doing) and unintegrated and formless (being). This is the realm of creative imagination and manifestation, the domain of free musical improvisation.

Chapter Five

Music as Mind: Playing

Before we make music, music makes us.
—George Leonard

Young children are natural improvisers. In his book *Frames of Mind,* Howard Gardner writes that musical intelligence is the first form of intelligence to emerge in the newborn.[1] The unborn child actually listens to musical and nonmusical sounds, starting at about the twenty-fourth week *in utero.* Music therapy research indicates that the fetus has distinct musical preferences. Once born, an infant actually shows recognition of the music that was played to him while in the womb. By the age of two months, some infants can match the pitch, loudness, and melodic contour of the their mothers' songs. At four months they can match rhythmic structure and engage in sound play that clearly expresses creative or generative properties. In the middle of the second year of life, babies improvise spontaneous songs that prove difficult to notate, along with characteristic bits from familiar tunes. Between the ages of three to four years, the young child begins to sing the songs that are popular in his or her social group. It is interesting to note that at around this age, the child's interest in improvisation and exploratory sound play generally fades. Gardner perceives this as a normal developmental dynamic, but I question his conclusion. Perhaps the child's interest in improvisation wanes because he is no longer encouraged to explore his inner world. It is noteworthy that around this time formal musical training begins for many children. If musical education does not include creative activities like improvisation, composing, musical imagination exercises, and moving with music (right-brain activities), along with technical left-brain training, it is likely that these more creative functions will move to the back burner of consciousness and eventually be forgotten.

Again, it is in the field of play and improvisation where we discover the self, which brings life, coherence, and meaning to the realm of mind. By encouraging only academic, technically correct musical expression in young children, we thwart their natural curiosity and creativity, their true power of manifestation in the world. I believe that this limited left-brain approach to music education has pushed many creative people away from developing their innate musicality. This is probably the main reason why many of us lose touch with our Essential Musical Intelligence. Improvising can help to bring it back.[2] The more you can give voice to the self through musical improvisation, the more the self comes alive and contributes to your vitality and wholeness.

The teenage years are a time for recapitulation of the important emotional learning that occurs in the transitional space of the young child. This developmental stage marks another perhaps more intense period of separation and individuation from parents. Trying on for size their newly acquired abstract-reasoning abilities, teenagers grapple with the endless emotional polarities that sprout from within and without. Add on the wildly fluctuating hormones circulating through their bloodstreams, and average teenagers find themselves with more than a full emotional plate. They question the nature of reality and constantly search for truth. Teenagers do seek out guidance during this turbulent time, but not from parents. They look for role models who speak their truth, ones who can validate their experience of chaos, confusion, and desire.

From the perspective of chakra psychology, the heart and throat chakras begin to open during adolescence. Teenagers grapple with intimacy issues, the pure passion of their emerging sexuality, and power and control identity issues. For many a sense of spiritual longing is activated. This is a time when music becomes an extremely important force in the teenager's life. Because they typically do not trust established institutions for spiritual and emotional guidance, they enlist in specific musical movements (hip-hop, alternative rock, gothic) to explore, celebrate, and worship a higher force and to receive the nurturance they need to move forward. Often teenagers idealize their favorite performers. For many, the idealized performer is cast in a hero role, which engenders a sense of hope, pride, and unconditional regard. This form of hero worship helps the teen to separate from his parents, as the idealization once reserved for them is now cast on a more emotionally accessible, age-appropriate role model.

A large number of creative individuals have reported that they began writing songs and poetry during this often disturbing, yet stimulating time in order to make sense of the contradictions in their lives. For them, writing music was a way to find their center, express their truth, and for some, the only way they felt they could be heard by significant others.

Many adults were denied the transitional space necessary to develop a stable, unique self-concept during their teenage years. Such people were probably narcissistically wounded early in life and have developed what Winnicott calls a "false self" that protects the real, vulnerable, creative self from being injured and betrayed by self-absorbed caretakers. Individuals with a false-self character structure feel isolated and unreal. Their authenticity was never seen or heard by the people closest to them who most likely imposed on them their own behavioral agenda. As children, these wounded individuals were acknowledged only when they were performing up to the standards of their caretakers. They often do not believe that they can be loved without proving themselves in some way.

In treating a number of anxious performers over the years, I have found that many were gifted children of narcissistic parents and were forced to develop the false-self character in order to remain in favor with parents and teachers. Most of these musicians have never improvised or approached music playfully. Many of them were forced to become adults at an early age and were never allowed to discover their uniqueness within their own transitional space. As they approached adolescence, these musicians found it too frightening to explore their true feelings. In addition, the conservatories they attended were performance oriented and did not encourage self-development through music. Hence, the word *performance* for me usually connotes a show, not necessarily something intimate, from the heart.

When these wounded musicians began to improvise as part of my group music-therapy approach, the light of self slowly began to melt the icy protective shields around their hearts. Within a matter of months, these musicians began to create the most delightful, sensual, powerfully original, and intimate music. They had awakened their Essential Musical Intelligence and found their true voices. One of the participants, an opera singer, brought in a vocal suite based on the poetry of Langston Hughes. This particular poem expressed quite poignantly the plight of the narcissistically wounded individual:

Heart

Pierrot took his heart and hung it on a wayside wall.
He said, "Look, passersby, here is my heart!"
But no one was curious. No one cared at all
That there hung Pierrot's heart upon the public wall.
So Pierrot took his heart and hid it far away.
Now people wonder where his heart is today.[3]

Musical improvisation is a way to reclaim the hidden heart, the voice of the self, the innocence of that unencumbered two-year-old who had no qualms about creating his own reality. Free improvisation is a natural conduit for your Essential Musical Intelligence. It allows for the expression of the Will of Nature, the movement of the soul in its desire to be known in human form.[4] Free improvisation is elemental; it does not involve the thinking mind. It is actually a state of no-mind that provides a perfect container into which obscure thoughts and feelings can be externalized and transformed through the symbolic language of music. One of the keys to transformation is your ability to surrender control and to cultivate an open, allowing attitude while experiencing the dynamics of your inner music. The second key is your ability to trust, through your relationship with EMI, that the music will take you where you need to go.

The following exercise will introduce you to the wonderful world of free musical improvisation and its role in facilitating healing and wholeness. Remember, you don't have to be a musician to create music; this ability is innate. The goal here is to surrender completely to the moment and create a musical self-statement, a snapshot of your inner life at this point in time, that reflects your cognitive and emotional states and your vitality affects. It may also expose internal conflicts and creative potentialities of which you are not yet even aware.

All you need is a variety of objects that make sound and rhythm. If you already play an instrument, feel free to use it. Most musicians that I have worked with, however, prefer instruments other than their primary one. Hand drums, recorders, *mbiras* (African thumb pianos), and other simple instruments can be wonderfully expressive. If you do not have access to instruments right now, be creative. Any object in your possession that makes a "joyful noise" (conch shell, washboard, a container of Tic-Tacs) will do).

I would even suggest that you begin to collect instruments for improvisation, particularly those to which you are spontaneously attracted. For example, African and Native American drums and rattles; old horns, guitars, and flutes; steel bundt-cake pans (they make a remarkable gonglike sound when struck), and Chinese gongs; crystal bell bowls and Tibetan temple bells. You can search for such items in ethnic stores, pawn shops, antique galleries and new-age shops. There are also commercial catalogues that sell reasonably priced instruments for music therapy practice. I list some of these companies in Appendix II.

Improvise Your Essential Musical Self-Statement

Once you have laid out your collection of instruments in a safe space where you will not be disturbed, take a moment to allow yourself to be drawn to one or more instruments. (It often helps to have a friend or two present who will reflect to you what he or she observes while you make your musical self-statement, although this is not necessary.) Be aware that impulses for improvisation are usually body-based, so you won't need your thinking mind for this exercise.

Place your instruments within comfortable reach and center yourself with the Breath Awareness exercise. When you feel ready, choose an instrument and allow an inner impulse to move through you and out via your hands or mouth. Listen to the melodies, rhythms, harmonies, and the expressive qualities (vitality affects) that you create. Surrender to the moment and let the music take you. (Remember, you need not be musically trained to practice this exercise.) Vitality affects are encoded at the core of your being and are naturally engaged whenever you open yourself to musical expression. Once you have made your essential self-statement, you will naturally stop playing. It is uncanny how this happens—the music just stops. It often feels like you have no control over this process.

Now take a few moments to reflect. Most people feel a wave of freedom, a sense of wholeness and deep fulfillment after making their musical self-statements. Some folks feel relieved that they could do it at all! What did you learn about yourself? Did you express a certain mood? Did you explore particular emotions? Did you become aware of internal conflicts? What did you learn about the music of your body? Why did you choose your specific instruments? Could playing them represent symbolically a means of fulfilling unmet instinctual needs? Be sure to record the answers to these questions in your Music and Sound Awareness Journal.

Improvisation gets us out of an analytical, doing-oriented left-brain mode and into the more global, emotionally labile right-hemispheric mode. Verbally processing the experience, however, allows both brain hemispheres to become integrated. When you can make sense of your emotional and intuitive experiences using your cognitive processing abilities, you are tapping into the highest level of emotional intelligence, which will ultimately lead to increased health, mind-body-spirit coherence, and well-being.

While demonstrating the above exercise for a group of students, I made an interesting discovery about myself. I had just spent much of the day writing and was delighted to come to class and play music. After describing the technique to my students, I was ready to demonstrate my musical self-statement. I chose an alto metallophone and a floor tom because I wanted to make a big sound. After centering myself, I picked up the beater for the metallophone and felt drawn to explore the sound of the beater on the wood around the metallophone. It sounded dull. I couldn't produce the rich, dark tone I wanted. I used every part of the stick and still couldn't find what I wanted. Finally, I was drawn to the floor tom, and I let my body unwind in a dancelike rhythm that soon sounded like a big, round, deeply rhythmic heartbeat. I felt powerful and wonderfully alive! For an instant it seemed that I had finished, but then I suddenly turned around and made one last loud thump on the drum. The students laughed. I wasn't sure at first what I had just expressed. After a number of insightful interpretations from the students, I finally began to understand.

I had recently noticed that it was difficult for me to dive into free musical improvisation after several hours writing at the computer. It was as if I were writing in New York and had to travel to Boston (a four-hour drive!) before I could sink into my usual deep level of musical communion. In other words, my attempts to create music after long periods of writing felt dull and uninspired. I had become quite frustrated, although I simply did not allow my feelings to surface. The musical self-statement reflected this sense of dullness when I first picked up the metallophone beater. It took a while to find my musical voice with the floor tom. Finally, I connected and felt a release, but then came the thump—the sound of my frustration surfacing. Perhaps I needed a witness (my students) in order to recognize the problem. I took the information to heart and was able to integrate more playing into days that were primarily focused on writing. Within a couple of weeks, I was back to my old comfortable level of musical expression. Remarkably, my writing also began to flow more easily when I integrated music breaks into the course of my day.

The musical self-statement exercise can also be used for exploring the emotional dynamics (inner music) underlying chronic physical problems.

Laura was a forty-five-year-old full-time secretary and former singer who had suffered chronic bladder infections for as long as she could remember. She regularly missed work because of the pain. She told me that her bladder was constantly expressing its presence in her life. Its lining was raw from constant infections and the side effects of medication. I asked Laura if anyone else in her family had experienced a chronic illness. She told me that her mother had had chronic bladder problems and had been hospitalized regularly when Laura was a child. Laura was not only abandoned by her mother at regular intervals during most of her childhood, she was forced to care for her four siblings while her mother was ill. She received no support from her father, a serious alcoholic. Laura was often overwhelmed and had no way to communicate her dilemma. She lived her entire life in survival mode and began getting bladder infections around the time her mother died when Laura was sixteen. She was tired of the pain and was ready to truly start living her life.

I asked Laura to tune into her Essential Musical Intelligence and to use the Six Steps to Healing to explore the inner music of her bladder. After affirming that her well-being truly mattered (step 2) and that she would be loved and protected during this exercise no matter what happened, she called upon her EMI for help (step 3). She then spent several moments tuning into the infinitely creative space of her throat chakra and waited for guidance (step 4). Laura was drawn to the Essential Musical Self-Statement exercise and searched for an instrument to match the voice of her bladder. She chose a conga drum. She began to play tentatively at first, but then proceeded to drum with great force in strong undulating rhythms. I supported her on a frame drum, creating a safe holding environment. After several minutes of intense drumming, Laura said that the pain had subsided and that her bladder felt calm, settled. She explained that she had actually been playing from her pelvis, not her arms, and that she had felt a lot of anger moving out through the music.

Laura next chose to tune into the lining of her bladder. She imagined it as raw and porous, unable to protect her from infection. First she chose the metallophone, but she could not find the right sound. Then Laura moved to the piano and began playing choppy chords up and down the entire length of the keyboard. Her playing was relentless, powerful, with an angry feeling tone. After a while, a shift occurred and Laura's playing changed. The chords now began to undulate like waves. Her improvisation ended with a lovely glissando up and down the keyboard. "This is the right sound," she said. "It could hold the voice of my bladder lining." Laura had released deep feelings of anger and resentment related to her childhood dilemma.

I asked her if she could listen for a sound to reflect the feeling tone of her bladder in its most whole and perfect state. Through the power of her intuition, Laura instantly connected with the vibration of the second chakra and intoned F above middle C with an OOH sound. She was moved by the power of the connection of the sound with her whole pelvic area. She began to breathe more deeply, and for a fleeting moment, imagined herself on stage singing (a previously unfulfilled desire). She felt a wave of hope permeating her being.

This story demonstrates the amazing effect of the unthought known on body, mind, and spirit. Laura literally internalized her mother's unthought known, which reflected vague unresolved issues around sexuality and creativity that were associated with the second chakra and manifested physically in the bladder. Because Laura was denied the normal experience of playing in her own transitional space both as a small child and as a teenager, she was unable to separate from her mother and continued to remain psychically attached (through her chronic illness) even after her mother died. Laura had split off her feelings of anger and resentment toward her mother in order to spare her mother additional pain and to protect herself from feeling guilty. It is my guess that the energy of these feelings fought for recognition by recreating the original childhood scenario (recurring bladder infections) and all the pain that went along with it. (Of course, there may have been a genetic predisposition as well.)

Laura confided that she had gone to many doctors and psychotherapists seeking a cure, but to no avail. It was clear to me that the problem, because of its roots in the earliest years of life (involving the mother-child relationship), would not be healed from the thinking mind or through palliative treatments. It had to be addressed at the level of Laura's inner music, her unthought known. During the process of EMI, Laura's engagement with music bypassed her cognitive processes and moved her directly into the emotional realm. She became aware of deep pockets of unexpressed anger in her pelvic area, some of which she was able to externalize through improvisation. It was interesting to note, in listening to Laura's musical expression, the change in vitality affects from choppy (angry) to undulating (calm, relaxed) over the course of the improvisation exercise. This, I believe, represented a tangible example of the alchemical force of Laura's Essential Musical Intelligence. Ultimately, the most important change to occur as a result of her engagement with EMI was Laura's resurrected desire to begin singing again, a healthy expression of both the second, third, and fifth chakras.

Relational EMI

Musical improvisation can also be used to explore relationship issues, which constitute a large portion of the pain that we experience at the level of mind. Many relationship difficulties stem from early family interactions. The memories from these early relational interactions are encoded in procedural memory (inner music) and cannot be accessed through verbal, cognitive processes. Again, music bypasses cortical functioning and goes directly to the emotional centers where the unexpressed feelings at the root of most relationship issues are harbored. Because music is a mirror of the inner life, when we improvise with two or more people, important inner dynamics are revealed. First of all, our inner music is externalized through our own musical expression; second, our true feelings toward the others will be expressed through the musical interactions; and third, in a group situation, we all take on a characteristic role (leader, follower, scapegoat) that is clearly articulated within the group process.

Marcia and Jonathan were grappling with intimacy issues. They had been together for seven years, and, though they loved each other very much, the fire had all but gone out in their relationship. Marcia, a successful stockbroker, felt that her husband was no longer interested in her sexually, and she was bitter and angry. Jonathan, a workaholic podiatrist, told her that he was just too exhausted for sex. They had talked for hours about the problem and spent a year in couples therapy trying to get to the root of Jonathan's avoidance behavior. When Marcia learned about EMI in one of my workshops, she decided that perhaps improvising together might be a way for her and Jonathan to experience greater intimacy in their marriage. Jonathan was somewhat intrigued with the idea, and together they chose a time when they would both be unhampered by work responsibilities. They gathered a bunch of instruments they had collected during their many trips abroad: a set of bongos, maracas, a tin whistle, Woodstock chimes, a small harp, and some claves (rhythm sticks). Neither Marcia nor Jonathan had any previous musical training, but both of them loved music. After centering themselves for a few moments, the improvisation began. Marcia seemed uncomfortable and picked up the claves and tentatively began playing a beat. Jonathan was like a kid in a candy store—he wanted to play each of the instruments and experienced great delight in his explorations. After a while, he noticed that Marcia's playing lacked energy, that she seemed depressed. He tried to engage her with a sexy beat on the bongos, but that closed her off even more. Jonathan went back to exploring the different instruments for several minutes while Marcia played a steady beat on the claves. She was the first one to stop playing.

In processing the musical interaction, Marcia realized that she was jealous that Jonathan had such passion for everything he did, including musical improvisation. She again questioned why he did not feel so passionately about her. Jonathan pointed out that she didn't really join him in the music making and that he had felt subtly controlled by her unchanging beat on the claves. He felt that he wasn't allowed to express the depth of his passion lest Marcia judge him. Marcia was surprised at Jonathan's revelation. She told him that, in fact, she admired his passion and wished that she were as creative as he. She admitted that sometimes she felt intimidated by him. Now it was Jonathan's turn to be surprised. He told Marcia that he felt like a failure sexually, that she had high expectations that he couldn't live up to.

It is fascinating how this simple musical interaction immediately exposed the root cause of Marcia and Jonathan's intimacy problems—performance anxiety. Both of them were afraid of expressing playfulness within the marriage for fear of being judged or rejected. These fears were probably rooted in some early painful childhood interactions that had never been fully processed or resolved; they were simply stored away in the personal unconscious. It would have been difficult for Marcia and Jonathan to deal with this problem in a verbal, analytic way. Instead, improvising music proved much more effective. Playing, as Winnicott taught, gives us permission to be creative, along with the opportunity to express ourselves from the level of self, as opposed to ego (where fear and doubt reside). And it is only from the level of self that we can express the deepest feelings of the heart, the real mind-body medicine.

Group Improvisation

The above musical improvisation exercise can be adapted for use in group situations as well. It works particularly well with families and other task-oriented groups, such as coworkers and sports teams. Musical improvisation groups typically consist of four to six players. Players are asked to choose from a variety of melodic and percussion instruments. The participants are encouraged to explore their relationship to their own music making and to other players without verbal communication. There are no other instructions.

Having witnessed and participated in numerous musical improv groups, it is paradoxical but true that almost all initial group improvisations tell a similar story. In the beginning of the improvisation, the music typically sounds chaotic and raw, with players expressing their unique moods, tonalities, and rhythms. At the midpoint, the chaos intensifies to an energetic climax, out of which a theme or dominant mood emerges. Participants continue playing together with one-pointed intention, exploring this theme or mood until they reach a resolution or conclusion. Each player then shares his or her experiences and impressions, followed by group discussion.

The improvisers are always surprised at how the music magically comes together without any discussion, and how they all spontaneously unite in a common feeling and purpose. Most participants report that out of the conflictual feelings and moods comes a meta-mood, one that provides a higher sensibility, a state of clarity and serenity. These qualities are end products of the transformational power of EMI.

For groups that grapple with ongoing power struggles or periods of stagnation and creative block, group improvisation is just what the doctor ordered. It provides a safe yet playful way to externalize, explore, and transform deeply rooted emotional issues that can be so burdensome—even destructive—if left buried within the group's unconscious.

Beloved composer Johann Sebastian Bach, an exquisite improviser himself, offered the following explanation of his use of music as a humane model for achieving harmony and coherence within the vast group musical improvisation of the human family:

> In the architecture of my music I want to demonstrate to the world the architecture of a new and beautiful social commonwealth. The secret of my harmony? I alone know it. Each instrument in counterpoint, and as many contrapuntal parts as there are instruments. It is the enlightened self-discipline of the various parts, each voluntarily imposing on itself the limits of its individual freedom for the well-being of the community. That is my message. Not the autocracy of a single stubborn melody on the one hand, nor the anarchy of unchecked noise on the other. No, a delicate balance between the two; an enlightened freedom. The science of my art. The art of my science. The harmony of the stars in the heavens, the yearning for brotherhood in the heart of man. This is the secret of my music.[5]

As you practice the EMI exercises in this chapter, your internal framework of reality will be challenged, and you might at times be overwhelmed by the onslaught of thoughts and feelings previously kept out of consciousness by your trusty defense mechanisms. Your defenses also operate unconsciously. You may be familiar with some of the more common ones described in psychology textbooks: repression, denial, projection, isolation, and reaction formation (when a painful feeling or idea is replaced in conscious awareness by its opposite). These defenses were quite naturally (and spontaneously) put into place in order to protect you from chaos and pain. In order to become whole, however, it is necessary to engage in a systematic loosening of defenses, many of which were erected when you were very young. By its very nature, music bypasses the defenses and leads directly to your inner world, where unresolved emotional conflicts, repressed memories, and archetypal material wait for the light of consciousness. As your ego expands and your connection to EMI deepens, you will find the confidence to allow more unconscious material—both dark and light—to enter consciousness to be transformed and integrated into your sense of self. Looking upon this expansion of self with an attitude of detachment and equanimity will do much to move this process along.

Often however, there are unintegrated parts of yourself that are invested in keeping you exactly the way you are. Generally these parts represent internalized, unevolved aspects of parents or other caregivers, known as introjects or split-off developmentally arrested aspects of yourself (subpersonalities), and they are threatened by change. The energy of these unintegrated parts is stronger than your rational conscious mind. Thus, they must be uprooted and welcomed into all decision-making processes that involve creative change. If you come across resistance to any of the exercises in this book, please read chapter 8 before you continue. This chapter explains the concept of personality fragmentation and the development of subpersonalities, and how to use your EMI to bring order, harmony, and safety to all parts of the self.

In the meantime, if you feel stuck and are unable to connect with your EMI, the following soul-song exercise provides an ego-based anchor when you feel temporarily lost in the sometimes stormy sea of self-transformation. Your soul song is a personalized chant that focuses on affirmation of self. It clarifies your sense of identity, your basic truths, and your personal mission in this life. It can be sung silently or full out any time you have a free moment—waiting for a bus, walking in nature, falling off to sleep, and especially during times when you feel out of balance, worried, or dejected. The song instantly connects you to your EMI.

Create Your Own Soul Song

To create your soul song, be clear in your intention to use this song to bring balance, joy, and healing into your life. Now begin to think about the lyrics of your soul song. Envision yourself in your highest mastery and create affirmations to express your ideal sense of self. Include personal goals as well as your most fervent spiritual desire. For example:

> I am a beautiful, loving woman,
> giving my musical gift to the world.
> I know that the spark in the heart of us all
> will bring us great joy if we just heed the call.

Next, choose a rhythm instrument. It could be a hand drum, a conga, bongos, or any other percussion instrument that will allow your own rhythm to emerge. Play until you discover a rhythmic pattern that feels right. Continue to play your rhythm until it is completely natural and steady. Then begin to listen for a melody to carry the lyrics you have created. If the lyrics don't fit the music, experiment until you find something that satisfies your soul. Make sure to record the process of creating your soul song so that you don't forget any of the vital verbal and musical information. You will know that your song is complete when singing it feels effortless. This is your song, the song that will be with you no matter what happens, the song that will remind you, even in your darkest hour, of who you are and your special purpose in this life.

This exercise works particularly well during transition: for example, when you are in the process of letting go of old, maladaptive habits and have not yet established yourself securely in more healthy ones. The Soul Song also helps tremendously when you experience fear and doubt with respect to your own self-worth or lose focus in the face of loss and disappointment. It also provides support when you are at a crossroad and feel confused about what direction to take. Your Soul Song can change and grow along with you. Feel free to edit or add new verses as you become more attuned to your true identity and mission in life.

As you practice the EMI techniques in this chapter, you will gain a large measure of control over the vicissitudes of your mental and emotional body. This sense of mastery increases your self-confidence and motivates you to explore the farther reaches of human nature. It also greatly increases the flow of energy in and through your mind-body. As your energy frees up and your mind becomes more still and harmonious, you may find yourself spending more time in the next higher level of consciousness, the intellect/intuition realm. Through your connection with EMI, you will explore the illusion of duality (the ego-based play of opposites and its ensuing conflicts), surrender to the wisdom and power of your intuition and imagination, and ultimately embrace the light of unitary consciousness, a state of creative manifestation, wholeness, and bliss.

Chapter Six

Music as Intellect/Intuition

Music is the mediator between the life of spirit and the life of the senses.
—Ludwig van Beethoven

Whenever you tap into the power of your Essential Musical Intelligence while practicing the exercises in this book, you are operating from the realm of intellect/intuition. This realm is the true home of your EMI. Using EMI is, in fact, a creative way to move your consciousness from the limitations of the mental-egoic plane to this next level. For instance, when you connect with the witnessing phase of EMI and become aware of the difference between the thoughts, feelings, and habits that are life giving and those that are depleting, you naturally develop your discriminative capacity. To know and then actively choose your highest good is associated with the intellect.

Your ability to trust that music will take you where you need to go during the transformational phase of EMI is associated with intuition. When you allow yourself to engage with this dimension, you naturally receive information directly from your higher self or soul, not from the fallible agencies of the senses or reason. Thus, the intellect/intuition realm contains both the dynamism of discrimination and will (intellect) and the quiet power of surrender and receptivity (intuition), two sides of the EMI coin. At the level of the intellect/intuition, you can now identify with a higher force within you that acts upon the mind, as opposed to being victimized by the dictates of your mind.

Archetypal Themes

As your mind becomes more still and the boundaries between conscious and unconscious are loosened, you can look at the core issues of your life with detachment and clearly see the archetypal and mythological themes being played out. This concept is most readily understood when viewed through the perspective of chakra psychology:

> The dramatizations of each chakra consist of a dance around a particular polarization and are based on an attempt to come to terms with a basic polarity in the world of names and forms, for each polarization creates an interaction, and the chakra is the focus of that interaction. At each chakra a primary archetype is expressed in the form of a dramatic representation. Each chakra has its unique scenario involving a

protagonist, a foil, and supporting characters. These parts have been enacted from time immemorial in myths, fairy tales, recorded history, and the theatrics of everyday life.[1]

The archetypal themes associated with each chakra were presented to you in chapter 3. Take a moment now to review them.

CHAKRAS AND ARCHETYPAL THEMES

Chakra	Model of Experience	Ideal Representations	Polarities
1. Root	Struggle for survival	victim	predator/prey, life/death
2. Sex	Sensory pleasure	hedonist	pleasure/pain, male/female
3. Solar Plexus	Mastery, domination, conquest, competition, inadequacy, inferiority, pride	hero	gain/loss, success/failure, dominance/submission, blame/praise
4. Heart	Compassion, generosity, selfless love, service	mother	rescuer/rescued, liberator/liberated
5. Throat	Devotion, receiving, nurturance and unconditional love, surrender, trust, creativity, grace, majesty, romance	child	object of mother/child, found/lost, trust/distrust
6. Third Eye	Insight, witnessing	sage	sage/fool, objective observer/deluded participant
7. Crown	Unitary consciousness	beyond form	none[2]

Paradoxically, the polarities represent both the root cause of human suffering and the path to liberation. A polarity involves extremes wherein one of the opposites is experienced as desirable while the other is judged as inferior and repulsive. Is there a particular polarity that resonates strongly in your own life right now?

Cynthia is a writer whose first novel catapulted her into the world of glamour and notoriety previously unknown to her. She enjoyed living the good life for several years until her money began to run out. She threw herself into writing her next book, which, after two years of hard work, received only lukewarm reviews. Another book followed that sold poorly. Though a brilliant writer and thinker, Cynthia began to doubt herself and her ability to earn a living through her creative work. Despising her newly acquired feelings of vulnerability and ordinariness, she fell into a deep depression. She desperately longed for the fame and fortune that once made her feel special and worthy. She became blocked and unable to resume writing.

Sound familiar? Cynthia's conflict embodies several classic archetypal polarities: success/failure, wealth/poverty, and doing/being. For Cynthia (and for most of us), success, wealth, and doing are desirable states, while failure, poverty, and just being are anathema.

From a transpersonal perspective, these opposites are just two sides of the same coin: you need to experience failure in order to appreciate success and vice-versa. According to the theory of opposites, the pure emotional energy associated with failure fuels creativity, which eventually allows for success, but feelings associated with failure (disappointment, anger, humiliation) must be fully experienced and not repressed or split off. (Note: Splitting is a defensive mechanism whereby the fragile ego, unable to hold the tension between two conflicting feeling states directed toward the same person, object, or event [love-hate toward performing], denies the more dangerous or inappropriate feeling state. This forbidden feeling is then split off and hidden from consciousness. Splitting, however, does not allow for normal synthesis between the two feelings, which creates an emotional block that prevents the individual from moving forward.)[3]

According to Hindu tradition, all polarities can be traced back to the two original polaric forces represented by the deities Shiva and Shakti. Shiva is the male principle representing pure unmanifest consciousness. Shakti is Shiva's female counterpart. She is the giver of life, the mistress of divine creation. Through union with Shakti, the consciousness of Shiva descends and imbues the universe with divine energy. Shakti represents the highest aspiration of the human soul. Her energy pushes up from the earth. The energy of Shiva is pulled down from the crown chakra above. Here we have a graphic depiction of the irresistible attraction of masculine and feminine energies that leads to creative manifestation. Mystics believe that it is

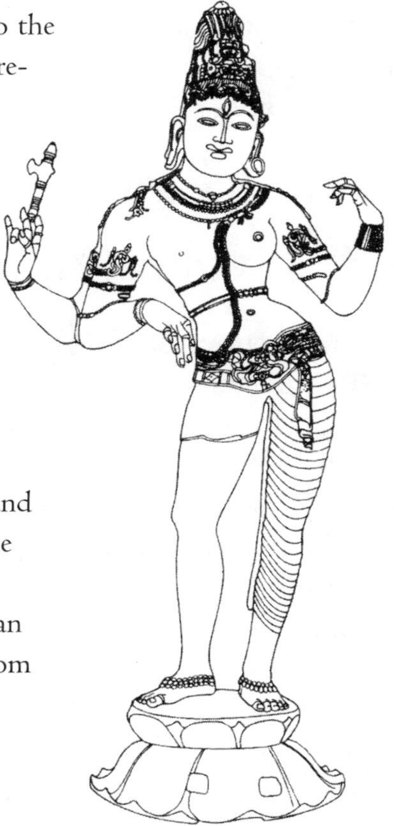

Shiva / Shakti:

Indicating right-left polarity and its relation to the male-female principles.

the eternal relationship of these two forces that comprises the phenomenal world.[4]

Sufi mystic and musician Hazrat Inayat Khan elucidates this concept in his book, *The Music of Life*: "The whole manifestation is duality, the duality that makes us intelligent. Behind the duality is unity. If we do not rise beyond duality and move toward unity, we do not attain perfection, we do not attain spirituality."[5]

As you become more comfortable traversing the terrain of intellect/intuition, you too will be directed toward the attainment of perfection and spiritual fulfillment.

Music as Archetypal Energy

Sound is the archetypal substrate of all life. The specific vitality affects expressed through music help to illuminate the human themes and associated emotions that unfold at each chakra level. Once these themes and emotions are brought to consciousness, music can assist you in resolving the inner conflicts stemming from the illusion of duality—the primary cause of human pain and suffering—and to recognize the Spirit permeating all life. As your consciousness becomes more centered at the level of intellect/intuition, you will soon experience what Kepler called the "music of the spheres," the harmony that permeates the universe. Music embodies this harmony and, within the context of EMI, becomes the catalyst for a harmonic framework within the body, mind, and spirit.

> The Pythagoreans define music as a perfect union of contrary things, unity in multiplicity, accord in discord. For music does not only coordinate rhythm and modulation, but puts

> order into the whole system; its end is to unite and to coordinate, as God also is the orderer of discordant things, and His greatest work is to conciliate among themselves, by the laws of music and medicine, things which are hostile one to the other.[6]

Musical Tantra: Reuniting Polarities

The wonderfully unique thing about music is that it can hold and express two conflicting emotions at the same time. Traditional Jewish *niggun*s (songs without words), for example, often evoke deep sadness and, at the same time, exuberance, joy, and hope. The blending of these conflicting energies produces a new, higher-level feeling state that is often difficult to describe in words. It is as if the music brings together the highest vibration in each emotion and out of their union, a third, more sublime meta-emotion is born.

This transformational aspect of music can be related to the Eastern art and philosophy of *tantra,* which the ancients described as the sacred dance of interpenetrating dualities. Proponents of tantra believe that duality, the first breaking of our initial unity, is a source of pain and alienation in life. Tantra is the yoga of reuniting duality, of restoring to oneness that which is separate. The result is an ecstatic experience of unity with ourselves, our partners, and the universe. The following Musical Tantra exercise is designed to help you use musical improvisation as a way of reuniting polarities. You can practice this exercise by yourself or with a partner. It can also be done with four people (two people playing each opposing self-state). Adding more players inevitably brings up interesting group dynamics that can enrich your experience of self-transformation and transcendence.

Musical Tantra

It is best, at first, to work with a partner in doing this improvisational exercise. Once you have discovered a core polarity, such as fear versus confidence, that you wish to explore musically, choose instruments that can express the energy of each opposing side. Next, choose the side (self-state) that has the strongest hold over you and improvise the feeling energy of this state as honestly and openly as you can. Surrender to the archetypal energy. At the same time, your partner will watch and listen carefully, since he or she will have to mirror this self-state later on. When the improvisation comes to a close, spend a few moments reflecting on what just occurred. What did you learn from this musical exploration? What were the musical qualities (vitality affects) of this particular state?

Next, clear yourself and tune into the other polarity. When you are ready, begin to explore the energy of this self-state. Let go and let the music take you where you need to go. When you have finished, allow yourself to get a sense of what was being expressed through the music. Note the differences between the two extreme states.

Now it is time for the transformational interaction between the two poles. Return to improvising the music of the first self-state while your partner imitates the music of the second state. Be true to each self-state but also maintain awareness of each other's music. Then let go and improvise freely.

> At some point during the improvisation, a shift occurs in which the two self-states come together and share core energies. Out of this musical communion, a new energy is born. This is the integrated state wherein lies your true power—the energy of your higher self that can infuse your life with a deeper level of understanding and enthusiasm.

Karen, an aspiring singer and songwriter, was grappling with the polarity of being unknown versus being famous. She chose the guitar (not her primary instrument) to express the music of being unknown. Her Unknown music sounded raw and vulnerable: dissonant, pained, unpredictable, but with a strong spirit, a bluesy quality that was earthy and quite moving. She described the music as sounding depressed, pessimistic, searching, having no value. She felt it communicated a feeling that nobody cared. Karen explained to me that she rejected this music—*and this aspect of herself.*

She then improvised the music of Fame. This music, also played on the guitar, sounded a bit manic. With its clear-cut melodic and rhythmic patterns, it seemed much more polished than the Unknown music, and it expressed confidence, sureness, an ability to reach everyone with joyous energy. The music said that she was good enough and that she was able to give something real—true happiness. Although this state was more desirable, the music lacked depth and grounding. We both heard that something was missing.

At this point, we were ready to explore the coming together of the two musical self-states. Karen, who identified more with the Unknown state, began to improvise this music, while I imitated her Fame self-state on another guitar. The duet was fascinating. As we played, the bluesy, Unknown music began to feed the somewhat vacuous music of Fame, which provided a sense of order and elegance. Interestingly, the Unknown music continued to imbue the Fame music with a deeply human quality that contained the primal voice and warming rhythms of someone who was in touch with core energies. Out of our musical interaction, a new music was born that drew from the highest aspects of each state and created a new entity—a nascent sense of self-worth and contentment—that reflected Karen's core essence and that helped to fill the raw, empty space between the two antipodal self-states.

Note: If you do not have a partner to play your opposing self-state, you can tape record yourself playing your less-dominant state. When you are ready for the two parts to come together, just improvise the music of the opposing part live while you play back the tape. Although the recorded music will not change (as it would if you were playing with a partner), it is still possible for you to access a higher state through your musical exploration.

In observing students engaging in the Musical Tantra exercise, many are initially loathe to spend time being with uncomfortable self-states such as stuckness and fear. Instead, students prefer the energy of change and confidence. They do whatever they can to avoid the former uncomfortable states. When they finally play the music of the weaker polarized state, they find that, although it may be difficult at first, there is much power in this state. The energy is raw, earthy, and deeply emotional, hearkening back to a time when life was less complicated and compartmentalized.

For example, four students decided to explore the polarity of stuckness versus change. Two of the women identified with stuckness and chose instruments to reflect this inner music. One sat down at the piano and repeated the same major triad over and over again in a slow, tedious manner, very cautiously inching her way up the keyboard. Her partner curled up on the floor to explore the springs on the underside of a snare drum, just being with the jagged sounds of the metal hitting the plastic drumhead. Both students were indeed expressing the energy of stuckness.

Meanwhile, the opposing team played the self-state they coined "Change." Both played drums, a large Irish frame drum called a *bodhran* and floor tom. Their music sounded frantic, intense, and powerful, and their expression was uninhibited and free. However, the music was manic and lacked direction. After about five minutes of the two teams playing seemingly independently, something began to shift. The pianist changed from major to minor, expressing a quality of pathos that was quite moving. The snare drum player began to sing a mournful song as she pulled at the metal spring, and at the same time, the drummers' frantic quality changed to a more grounded, supportive energy. They were receiving the pain of stuckness, which gave them a reason to help facilitate change. The Stuckness players opened to the radiant confidence of the drummers and integrated this quality into their expression. A new powerful music ensued that melded the two forces and produced the sound and feeling of serenity. Everyone could feel the change and after a few minutes, the music naturally came to a close. This musical encounter provided the direct experience of resolving the polarity of stuckness versus change. The resulting state of serenity will remain a guiding force in their lives.

In practicing this exercise yourself, once you have heard, experienced, and embodied the new music that represents the resolution of opposite poles, it is important to integrate this quality into your daily life and to seek this state of balance as much as possible. For example, when the aggressive yet empty pull of fame tugs at Karen's consciousness, she now remembers the feeling state of self-worth and contentment, which brings her back to center.

This state of mind allows Karen to be prepared for success and thereby naturally attract more attention and fame.

When you find yourself caught in a polarity, remember your Essential Musical Intelligence and explore the musical and emotional dynamics of each pole without judgment. You will know experientially that one side of the polarity is no better or worse than the other; both are necessary for true growth. Through completely embracing each pole and allowing them to come together creatively for your highest good, you will move to the next level of consciousness, a state of nonduality and true freedom. Musical Tantra teaches you to accept not only all aspects of yourself, but also people you avoid because of irreconcilable differences—your shadow counterparts. These difficult individuals often carry a split-off part of yourself. It is worth your while to explore why. Transforming polarities through the practice of EMI is the quickest solution for peace both within and without. We are, in essence, all united. Your Essential Musical Intelligence will lead you to this realization.

The Drama of the Gifted Child

Polarity extremes are common in people who have been narcissistically wounded as children. Children are naturally intuitive and deeply connected to the life of the soul. When their soul qualities and special gifts are not acknowledged and encouraged by loved ones, or worse, if they are shamed, humiliated, or exploited when they express these qualities, children may develop false selves to protect the precious true self that lies at their core. The false self behaves "appropriately" so that the child will not be criticized or abandoned.[7] Although tragic, the development of a false self is the child's sophisticated and brave attempt at survival. Splitting (denying true feelings and desires) becomes the raison d'être of these children, and where there is splitting, there is deadness. The soul goes into hiding and only the extremes of polarity are left.

Steve, a thirty-five-year-old party planner, had been living a false-self reality for as long as he could remember. It was not until he explored the emotional polarities in his life through the Musical Tantra exercise that he discovered his true self and experienced deep fulfillment and joy in daily life. As a boy, Steve was ebullient, wildly creative, and gifted in music and art. He was the oldest son of puritanical parents who felt they had to break Steve's spirit in order for him to be a productive, law-abiding citizen. He was forced to work in the family business from an early age, so there was not much time for him to develop his creative talents. Because he was restricted from playing freely and expressing himself, work became a joyless exercise of being compliant, productive, and plodding through the day. Play, on the other hand, was associated with what Steve called "the grand gesture," a fantasy world where everything was exciting, lavish, perfect. A major polarity for Steve was work and suffering versus escape into fantasy, where he could create a glamorous world of beauty and perfection. Unfortunately, in either state, he could never relax and just be. In practicing the Musical Tantra exercise, Steve represented these states on the piano with "plodding" music—loud, thick angry chords spread out between his two hands that moved relentlessly up and down the keyboard—and grand-gesture music—light, airy glissandos played mostly in the higher register of the keyboard. Both these extreme states caused Steve emotional pain. Essentially, he was driven by his false-self persona and was unable to derive pleasure from either work or play.

After about a year of working with EMI and playfully introducing the freedom and spontaneity of the grand gesture to the logic and persistence of the plodding self-state through musical improvisation and in his everyday interactions, Steve was finally able to find the integration point—his true voice. It happened one day after a particularly grueling business meeting. Steve returned home exhausted and disillusioned. He walked directly to his piano, sat down, and placed his hands on the keys, breathing calmly and rhythmically, and waited. After what seemed an eternity, he finally played one note. This note led Steve to the next note and then the next. In a matter of moments, a haunting melody sprang from the depths of his being, expressing pure vulnerability and raw beauty. Steve explained, "One could get lost in the pregnant space between each note." This was the sound of Steve's Essential Musical Intelligence. Out of those spaces emerged the voice of Steve's real self. For the first time, he was able to hear and feel his innate divine essence.

From that day forward, Steve has allowed his real self to guide him in creating an integrated lifestyle that truly works for him. He has drawn closer to nature and has bought a house on Martha's Vineyard. Once there, he realized how much he loves the simple, peaceful island life. He revived an old dream of owning an antique store, and bought an aging garage on the island, which he began to fix up. He then took delight in traveling the world to collect antiques for his new shop. In about a year's time, he moved his life and business to the island full time. Here he truly enjoys the integration of work and play and has become quite successful in his antique business. In this peaceful, relaxed, exuberant state, he soon met the partner of his dreams and has finally been able to share his heart with another. Through engaging his EMI and resolving painful polarities through Musical Tantra, Steve's life has become like music itself—harmonic, flowing, symmetrical, and free.

Child-versus-Adult Polarity

People with early narcissistic wounds frequently suffer from the child-versus-adult polarity. In working with these folks, I often find that either the child-self was parentified and cut off from innocence and play like Steve, or was never allowed to grow up, individuate, and gain true power in the world (the plight of many gifted musicians). Both states necessitate the development of a false-self constellation, which is extremely stressful and alienating for the child, and creates the basis for later depression, somatization, and addiction.

In exploring this polarity through the Musical Tantra exercise, you may discover that the adult child's music is typically innocent, playful, unselfconscious, and autisticlike in its concentration. The adult's music is more structured and regular and exhibits an air of responsibility, altertness, correctness, and control. In interacting with the child music, you can sometimes hear the adult's frustration and impatience with the occasional oblivion of the child. As the adult's music merges with the child's, however, it becomes more free and expressive. Likewise, the child soaks up the structure, stability, and support of the adult. The result is integration of the brain hemispheres and higher-level functioning.

For example, in observing a student's Musical Tantra exercise, I noticed that the child player moved from using only one hand on the piano, which expressed a sense of fragility and isolation, to using both hands independently (during interaction with the adult music). This mirrored integration of her brain hemispheres, which facilitated a highly creative state that allowed her to improvise a poignant song about her early troubled family life.

The student told me that this was the first time that she had allowed her inner child to share her story with outsiders. The musical interaction fostered a corrective emotional experience for the child player that allowed her to make peace with the previously toxic adult self-state and to own her power as an integrated being.

In engaging in the Musical Tantra exercise, you will directly experience music as an archetypal blueprint for harmony—a channel for your soul's perfection to be manifested in human form. Please note, however, that deep and lasting change occurs only if you integrate the qualities of the new higher level into your daily life. Once this new orientation, or soul state, is awakened and realized, you cannot go back again. You must let it grow.

Musical Tantra Diagram

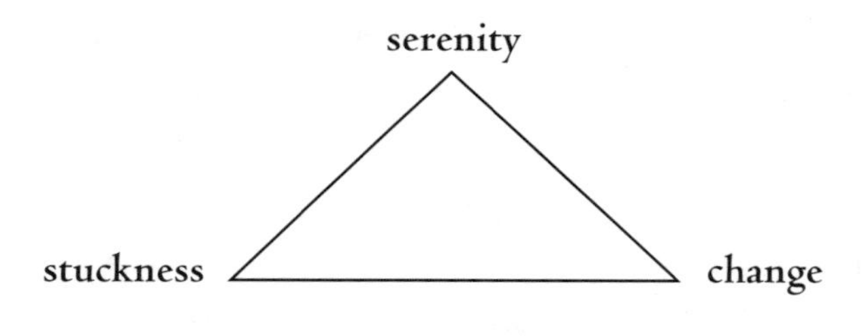

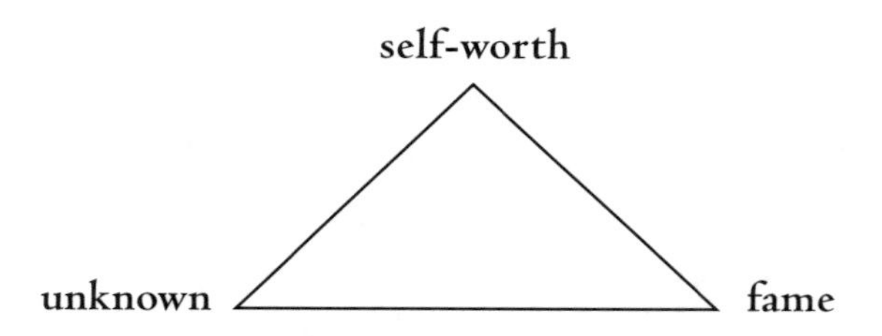

EMI and the Imaginal Realm

The stronger the imagination, the less imaginary it is.
—Rabindranath Tagore

At the level of intellect/intuition, you have easy access to the stream of your imagination, the magical state between waking and dreaming, the realm of creativity and transformation. In this context, it is useful to think of the imagination as the intermediary state between heaven (pure consciousness or bliss) and earth (mind, body, and ego). At this level of being, you gradually realize that you are the creator of your own life. It then becomes necessary to take responsibility for your unique creation by monitoring your thoughts, words, beliefs, and actions. Through awakening your EMI and using it as a bridge to connect the higher reality (intuitive wisdom) with the earth plane (sensory and ego-based thoughts, feelings, and memories), you can literally create heaven on earth and manifest balance and harmony in your life.

Prayer, affirmation, and visualization are creative tools that can help to bridge this gap, whether they are used with music or not. One prayer in particular mirrors the resolution of polarity through surrender to transcendent reality. This is the prayer of St. Francis of Assisi. This prayer can provide an anchor for you as you climb the slippery slope toward nonduality:

Prayer of St. Francis of Assisi

Lord, make me an instrument of your peace.
Where there is hatred, let me sow love;
Where there is injury, pardon;
Where there is doubt, faith;

Where there is despair, hope;
Where there is darkness, light;
And where there is sadness, joy.

Lord, grant that I may not so much seek to
be consoled as to console;
To be understood, as to understand;
To be loved, as to love.
For it is in giving that we receive,
It is in pardoning that we are pardoned,
And in dying that we are born to eternal life.

The problem with many people in "dying," or surrendering to self, is the feeling of lack or emptiness. Many people accumulate things in order to feel full or realized. The inability to realize our fullness from within is the main cause of most addictions. We become dependent on a substance to push away the gnawing emptiness that is simply a blanket covering our EMI. In psychoanalytic literature, music is associated with orality, a kind of psychic feeding, a filling up with spirit. Music can be used to create this state of fullness and abundance both within and without. From an Eastern perspective, music is spirit, Shakti, the original creative energy. In ancient spiritual traditions, when the priest or shaman used music to invoke the favor of the gods, he or she was almost certain to receive what was desired. Music was a form of prayer, sung from a place of integration—the rational, linear left brain and the intuitive, receptive, emotionally alive right brain working together in the spirit of devotion and surrender to divine will. Music carries the healing message and infuses it with the creative aspect, which is why chanting is so powerful. The ancient archetypal frequencies, which were revealed to the mystics and prophets who came before us, enable our higher reality to be embodied in human form.

Again, music is the archetypal framework of all life. As Hans Jenny showed us, sound moves matter. Depending upon what we actually sing about, we create either harmony or chaos. For example, Billie Holiday sang songs about being mistreated and abandoned by men, as did Janis Joplin. Their life histories reflect tremendous pain in intimate relationships. As in life, so in music, or vice-versa? What about Tupac Shakur, Biggie Smalls, and Kurt Cobain? All three continually sang about death and destruction. Could their choices of music have actually led to their demise? On the other hand, Hindu saint Anandamayi Ma constantly chanted the name of God. She became a radiant being who brought healing to millions.

Take a look at the songs that you most identify with at this point in your life. Most likely these songs reflect different aspects of your being—unresolved conflicts from the past, present desires and dreams, and wishes for the future. If you find that you are fixated on listening to or singing one particular kind of song—for example, all blues, or all death metal—it might be helpful to explore your attachment to the content of these pieces. You are probably stuck in an unresolved complex or negative pole of a chakra dramatization. Exploring this polarity through Musical Tantra or expressive therapy could lead to greater clarity and diversification of your musical choices and life energies. It is important for you to be conscious of what you sing and listen to. We create what we focus on.

EMI Abundance Song

As you can see, music intensifies the power of the imagination. By combining imagination, affirmation, and music, you can create your own healing songs to manifest greater abundance in all areas of your life. In order to write a meaningful song, however, there must be coherence between both hemispheres of the brain. One of the main reasons we don't receive what we ask for is incongruence between our thinking and feeling regarding the object of desire. Creating an abundance song gives you an opportunity to explore each aspect (ego versus soul desire; what you think you need versus your highest good) and bring them together in a way that gets you what you want.

Take a few moments now to think about something that you really want to create in your life. It could be something material, like a new car or apartment, or better health, or a healthy intimate relationship. Following are two ways to create your song. Choose the one that is most comfortable for you.

Create Your Own Abundance Song

Let the image of what you want to create connect with the feeling of desire located in your solar plexus. Now allow an affirmation to spring forth that captures the essence of your desire and expresses it powerfully and succinctly, such as, "I have a new large, bright, airy, serene apartment that allows me to live comfortably and happily and provides a safe place to fulfill my creative dreams." Finally, create melody and a beat to provide a musical framework for your new Abundance Song. Record it, memorize it, and repeat it with sincere enthusiasm as often as possible. It will lead you to the quickest route to manifest your heart's desire.

Another way to create your Abundance Song is to

center yourself fully in the image and feeling of living with what you desire. Then improvise a spontaneous song about having it. You can do this a capella or with harmonic and rhythmic accompaniment. Be sure to record this music so that you can refine and memorize it. If the improvisation is too long and cumbersome, you can extract the most relevant lines and fashion them into your Abundance Song.

Sean sang about having a new musical career as a solo artist rather than his usual job as a sideman. He sang, unaccompanied, about having the courage to express the music of his heart to thousands of listeners, of the joy he would feel when fans sang along with him in concert, about the money he would earn and his pleasure in spending it. He radiated joy and enthusiasm as he improvised his song and later told me that deep inside he knew that what he was singing was true and would manifest in due course. He later highlighted the most powerful lines of the improvisation and crafted them into a song that he sang twice daily for several months. In about a year's time, I witnessed a wonderful transformation in this young man's life. His Abundance Song became a reality.

The Abundance Song can also be used to create a significant change in health status. Erika, who had recently had a miscarriage and was pregnant again, created an Abundance Song to ensure the health of her baby:

My Uterus

my uterus is strong and healthy
my uterus is whole

it's a cradle for my baby
it's a place she can call home

my uterus is strong and healthy
like a fortress in a storm
standing *fortiter et recte*
it will never let me down
my uterus is divine

When creating an Abundance Song, you may encounter resistance from uncooperative subpersonalities who are threatened by the possibility of change.

Georgia wanted a million dollars in venture capital to start a new technology business. She had never owned a business before but felt she was ready to strike out on her own. As she started to sing about having the money, she felt blocked. The thought of getting a million dollars brought up intense fears of responsibility. Georgia didn't know how she could manage all that money. As she explored her fear, she was met with the polarity of adult versus child. She used the Musical Tantra exercise to explore each pole, and soon realized that she felt disdain for the adult part of her who could be wise and responsible. This part was associated with greed, control, and bitterness. It was a part she avoided. The child part, however, was vulnerable and needy, Georgia's usual state of being. It took a while for her to separate her distorted image of the adult from its pure state and to allow her child self to be supported and guided. When the integration of the two states finally occurred, Georgia created her Abundance Song. The song provided a framework for empowerment whereby she could create a business plan to attract venture capitalists. In less than six months, she was well on her way.

If you would like to create a musical accompaniment to support the development of your Abundance Song, the following practical tools may be helpful:

1. Create a simple *harmonic vamp* on a piano, autoharp, or guitar. The easiest and most effective vamp is a hymnlike *A-men* in the key of C, an F-major triad moving to a C-major triad over the span of two measures (four-four time) in a kind of slow to medium tempo. Each phrase of your song should last for one complete exhalation.

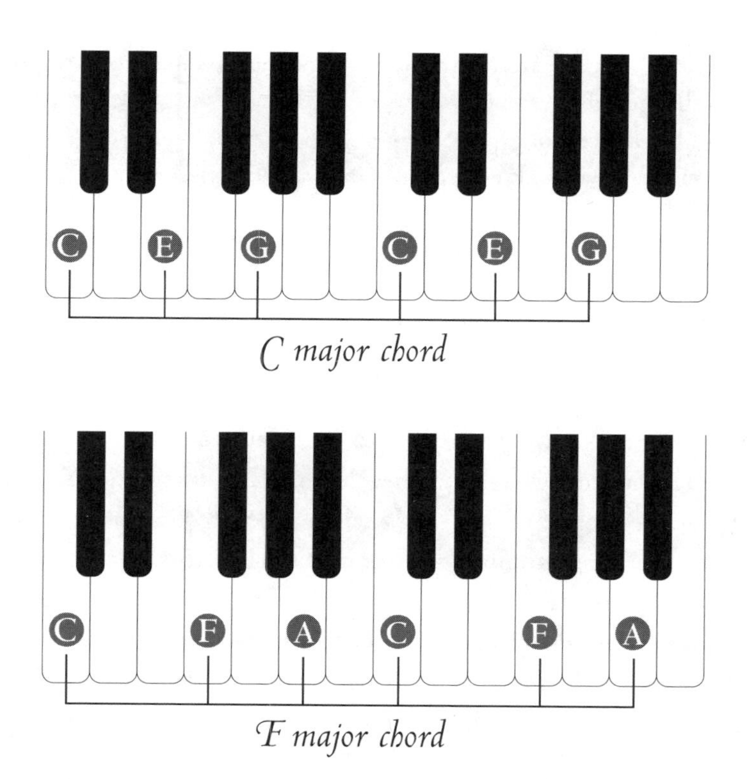

2. Create a simple *rhythmic groove* with a set of bongos, a rhythm egg, or claves. The rhythmic groove lends a sense of structure, continuity, and security as you work with both your crafted song or your free improvisation. You can use a drum machine

or Rap Master for creating complex rhythmic grooves—the more syncopated, the better. You can also borrow a groove from your favorite hip-hop or smooth-jazz group. Use your improvisation instruments to recreate this groove, record it, and then sing your abundance song over it. The most important thing is to keep the rhythm steady so that your improvisation has a solid ground.

Record your Abundance Song, listen to it regularly, work with the key lines (the ones that draw the most emotional energy), refine it, and repeat it as much as possible. Repetition creates changes in your unconscious mind. You can also listen to your Abundance Song prior to going to sleep at night so that its message will sink even deeper into the unconscious mind.

The Intellect/Intuition Paradox

From time immemorial, mystics, visionaries, and seers of various religions have attempted to elucidate the experience of the intellect/intuition realm, the domain of transcendent reality. What these great teachers inevitably discovered, however, was that when the mind attempts to reason about spiritual matters, it necessarily generates paradox, because spirit is beyond the mind. Thus, linear left-brain symbolic language may not be the best choice in exploring this imaginal realm. Proponents of Eastern philosophies advise bypassing language when attempting to achieve higher states, since language binds the conscious mind into dualism. Communication theorist and educator Marshall McLuhan is right when he says:

> The next logical step would seem to be, not to translate, but to bypass language in favor of a general cosmic consciousness

> [which] might be very much like the collective unconscious . . . The condition of "weightlessness," which biologists say promises a physical immortality, may be paralleled by the condition of "speechlessness" that could confer a perpetuity of collective harmony and peace.[8]

Music is transsymbolic. Because it offers immediate nonconceptual insight, it is the perfect medium with which to navigate the imaginal realm. As you engage more and more with your Essential Musical Intelligence, whose true domain is the active imagination, you will be graced by the numinous feeling that you are nearing the resolution of polarity, and in this state, anything can happen—even miracles. Visionary physician Larry Dossey writes about the two major domains of healing: first, the rational/doing therapies (medication, surgery) whose results are explained by science; and second, the paradoxical/being therapies, whose results seem to arise out of nowhere.[9] It is in this paradoxical domain that we witness the extraordinary effectiveness of EMI in healing body, mind, and spirit.

The main paradox that we experience at the intellect/intuition level is the need to surrender to a higher power while taking full responsibility for our own psychospiritual growth. It is a slippery slope where we place ourselves in God's hands, yet remain ever vigilant in choosing efficient, healthy behaviors, thoughts, and feelings. It is at this level that we realize we are in partnership with our higher selves. Here we learn to become witnesses to the archetypal dramas of our lives, while at the same time calling for a deeper connection with our true life purpose. Usually we reach this level of consciousness only after trials and tribulations that leave us weary and skeptical. We want to finally get off the roller coaster and create a more stable reality. Another helpful prayer, this one from the Hindu tradition, can facilitate this choice:

The Guru Prayer

Lead me from the unreal to the real.
Lead me from darkness to the light.
Lead me from mortality to immortality.

Music, Symbols, and Altered States

The realm of the intellect/intuition is the domain of the imagination. The most effective way to access this realm is through changing our brain waves from our more normal states of consciousness (*beta,* thinking; and *alpha,* relaxed concentration) to *theta,* the hypnogogic state, also known as an altered state of consciousness. This transitional dreamlike state normally occurs just as we are about to fall asleep and as we awaken from sleep. The theta state can also be induced through deep relaxation, hypnotic entrainment, shamanic drumming, and, of course, through intentional music listening and improvisation.

When you externalize the truth of your being through musical improvisation (as you did in the Musical Tantra exercise), you naturally operate out of the theta state. Here you have direct access to the personal and the collective unconscious. At the collective level, you receive archetypal symbolic messages that can help to expand your reality and give you more energy for creative growth. You can also effectively plant healing seeds through affirmation and visualization that can change the direction of your life.

Of course, when functioning at the theta level, you are also privy to the darkest, most repressed material. As you may have experienced while practicing the Musical Tantra exercise, it is often this dark, split-off material (memories, feelings, desires) that holds much of your power. When both light and dark material are viewed from the level of the intellect/intuition, however, you eventually realize that each complements the other and can be neutralized or transformed through your Essential Musical Intelligence. The daily practice of meditation or self-hypnosis can help you immeasurably in realizing this advanced state of equanimity.

The imagination is both factory and warehouse for archetypal symbols that function as accumulators, containers, preservers, and transformers of dynamic psychological energies. They are the building blocks of creative manifestation. Take a few minutes now to reflect upon the symbols that have special meaning for you (sun, moon, trees, power animals, religious deities, castles, money). When you consciously visualize a symbol, it sets in motion unconscious psychological processes.

For example, visualizing a rose is often associated with opening the heart chakra and feelings of awe, perfection, and unconditional love. The more time you spend visualizing the rose and opening to its symbolic message, the greater the impact it will have on your consciousness. You may realize that you can allow the light of your higher self to open the petals around your heart chakra so that your inner beauty is revealed. (This is tremendously healing, especially if you have suffered hurts and have built a self-protective wall around your once-trusting heart.) By visualizing symbols and internalizing their meaning and power, you can achieve further integration between the conscious and unconscious elements of your personality and between the two hemispheres of the brain.

Listening to music in an altered state of consciousness is an effective and enjoyable way to explore the imagination. In this deeply relaxed state, archetypal messages encoded in music and sound come alive in the form of symbols, feelings, memories, and images that can lead you to deeper levels of self-awareness and transformation. When listening to music in an altered state, you can watch the images unfold, feel their impact on your consciousness, and, as in lucid dreaming, change the scenarios if you wish. In trusting the intelligence aspect of EMI, however, it is best to surrender to movement of the symbolic material evoked by the music (as opposed to manipulating it) and let it take you where you need to go.

The following exercise uses the framework of the six-step process of activating EMI to help you enter an altered state of consciousness and use music to evoke imagery to expand your consciousness and facilitate healing.

Magical Musical Imagery

1. **Identify the problem.** Determine what you would like to explore. This could include generalized topics such as expanding awareness, appreciating nature, a quiet place, or creative change; or more specific problems like loneliness, mourning, or a difficult relationship. You could also explore specific issues related to chakra polarities, like the hero's journey, devotion, mastery, compassion, or pleasure seeking. (Warning: Since you will be in a deeply relaxed and open state, do not attempt to explore traumatic issues. It is best to work with these under the guidance of a trained therapist.)
2. **Remember your true worth.** Affirm that you are worthy of higher states of consciousness and resolving your problem. Know that no matter what comes up during this exercise, you will be lovingly held by the music and guided toward your highest good.

3. **Become proactive.** Once you have decided upon the scenario or issue that you want to explore, select music that embodies the emotional charge, energy/breath patterns, and chakra elements related to that issue. You can use the methods for musical selection described in chapter 3: the energy/breath circuits or the five-element chakra theory. In finding the most appropriate music for the Magical Musical Imagery exercise, it is usually more effective to choose instrumental music, which reflects pure archetypal energies without mental input, as opposed to songs with lyrics. Classical music works quite well for evoking imagery, particularly program music (Franck, Tchaikovsky, Mahler, Sibelius), music from the Romantic period (Chopin, Schumann, Schubert, Mendelssohn), music that evokes strong emotional reactions (Brahms, Stravinski, Wagner), and music with folk elements (Messiaen, Bartok). Certain types of new-age music (Kitaro, Yanni, George Winston) can also create the experience of spaciousness for inner travel and exploration. Once you have selected one or more pieces of music (make sure you have enough to last between twenty and forty minutes), program them in their appropriate order on your CD player or make a separate disc or tape. An example of music for an imagery session that reflects polarities in the heart chakra might be Dvorak, Largo, from Symphony No. 9; Vaughan Williams, Dives and Lazarus; and Mahler, Adagietto, from Symphony No. 5. (See Appendix III for suggestions.)

4. **Connect with your throat chakra.** Once you have selected your music, tune into your center of receptivity and expression. Feel that you are opening to the guidance of your higher self and affirm that you will let the music guide you.

5. **Express yourself.** The following is adapted from the "Guided Imagery and Music" method developed by music therapy pioneer Dr. Helen Bonny.[10] To begin, find a quiet, secluded spot where you will not be disturbed for at least an hour. With your remote control device close by, lie down and deeply relax each part of your body from head to toe. Once you are very relaxed, count down from ten to zero. Each time you count back, you will feel more and more relaxed. When you reach zero, you will feel profoundly relaxed.

   For example: Ten . . . I am feeling more and more relaxed. Nine . . . I am calm. Eight . . . I am relaxing deeper and deeper. Seven . . . calm and peaceful. Six . . . more peaceful and calm. Five . . . I am heavy, warm, and comfortable. Four . . . more and more relaxed. Three . . . I am feeling very quiet. Two . . . muscles like jelly. One . . . going deeper and deeper. Zero . . . profound relaxation.

   Imagine that you are lying in a beautiful meadow. Feel the texture of the cool grass beneath you; take in the wonderful sounds of chirping birds and whispering wind; feast your eyes on the clear blue sky and green foliage. When you sense that you are fully engaged with the meadow, ask for a symbol that will bring you more power and clarity in manifesting the next step on your healing path. Now turn on the music.

The music will usually activate your visual imagination, but not always. Some people experience only kinesthetic sensations or strong emotions in an altered state. This symbolic material is equally important. Allow yourself to stay with the experience and see how it unfolds. When a particular symbol appears on the screen of your imagination that has special meaning for you, interact with it playfully and simply observe what happens. You might want to engage in a dialogue with the symbol. With the innate structure of the music supporting you, ask your symbol to reveal its truth. If it takes you to a place that is frightening or uncomfortable, you can easily bring yourself back to ordinary reality by opening your eyes and using the breath to center yourself.

When the music is over, come back the same way you entered the altered state, bringing with you any relevant symbolic material. Gently wiggle your fingers and toes, rub your hands together and cover your eyes, slowly open them into your hands, and allow yourself to connect with ordinary reality. Have crayons and fourteen-by-seventeen-inch drawing paper nearby. Draw a large circle and fill it in with the images or symbols that you brought back from your journey.

6. **Give thanks.** Spend some time processing your experience by writing down any significant insights in your Music and Sound Awareness Journal. Acknowledge the power of your Essential Musical Intelligence as a transformational bridge connecting your inner and outer worlds.

When practicing the Magical Musical Imagery exercise, significant themes often emerge. For example, Constance, an experienced traveler in the symbolic realm, felt lost after a painful breakup with her long-term boyfriend. She wanted to explore this feeling state using the Magical Musical Imagery exercise. She chose *Inner Vistas* (Sacred Spirit Music), etheric music played on gongs, bells, and tambura. This composition, which is more like landscapes of sound rather than music, embodies the vastness of space. It has no particular melody or harmony, which leaves lots of room for images to emerge.

During the first few minutes of listening, Constance experienced some physical pain in her pelvic area. Once the music was over, she began to create her mandala. Tears welled up in her eyes and she sobbed, "I don't want to be alone." She realized that the pelvic pain reflected a recurring conflict related to fear of abandonment (second chakra). She explained that the music helped her to get in touch with a heavy sense of being alone in space. Her imagery was of a "weird, alien, glass world" that she experienced as scary and painful. She had tried to avoid entering this world by constant involvement in relationships in which she merged with her partner and lost herself.

When you engage in the Magical Musical Imagery exercise, you allow the music to externalize whatever is up for you at that moment. The music took Constance where she needed to go on her healing path. She explained further, "The pain allowed a part of me to be born—a desire to give from a place of power. But first, I had to find my own power." As the music continued, Constance explained that a new kind of symbol emerged: water, nature, memories of Topanga Canyon (a safe place for Constance), a lion lying down with a lamb, a full womb ready to give birth. She placed these and other significant symbols in her mandala, using only orange-red and purple crayons. Once she finished drawing the symbols, she connected the color purple (which represented her ego) with orange-red (representing earth), which, when blended together, created the color brown. This color allowed Constance to feel integrated and grounded. Brown, for Constance, contained all colors, which created in her the sensation of fullness.

When we surrender to the Magical Musical Imagery exercise, the music usually brings up symbols that reflect the work we need to do and the archetypal beings and objects that can be a source of guidance and transformation. We receive power and energy from our internal symbols—water, power animals, specific colors, mountains, and archetypal characters. The first time I practiced this exercise, I was greeted by an image of the Divine Mother, a radiant figure who filled the entire expanse of my inner screen with a powerfully warm, nurturing, loving energy. My body pulsated with the vibrancy of the image. The actual feelings of expansiveness, love, awe, and safety stayed with me long after the journey was over and continues to enhance my life whenever I recall it.

The Magical Musical Imagery exercise is not complete until you process the experience through mandala drawing, musical improvisation, movement, or poetry. If you are artistically inclined, the mandala is a powerful way to process the experience. *Mandala* means "center, circumference, or magic circle." Carl Jung associated the mandala with the self, the center of the total personality. He suggested that the mandala exhibits the natural urge to live out our potential, to unfold the pattern of our whole personality.

During the Magical Musical Imagery exercise, the music opens the door for you to actively engage with the archetypal realm. Later, by externalizing through mandala drawing what you have discovered in this formerly unknown place, you actually create a living container for these deeper contents of self to unfold and develop. The mandala, as a circle itself, is symbolic. It represents a tangible transformational space where you can just be, as well as a place you can return to in order to continue to explore and unravel symbolic meanings.[11]

In describing the aftereffects of the musical imagery exercise, Constance reported that she was able to make great strides in dealing with her fear of being alone. "I became full with myself through this exercise. I don't want to relate to any man from that place of icy coldness and emptiness . . . I realized that in my last relationship, I couldn't have the real deal because I was so desperate . . . I integrated the mountain range, stars, diamond flowers, and the lion with the lamb into the center of my being. All those images merged into an electric baby of creativity."

The image of the electric baby represented the Divine Child who is unconditionally loved and nurtured and who will connect Constance with an eternal source of love and guidance from her higher self. Through contacting her Essential Musical Intelligence with the Magical Musical Imagery exercise, Constance began to fill herself with soul energy, the most effective ingredient for transforming inner emptiness.

Self-transformation is a long and sometimes arduous path. Transforming habits and detaching from ego concerns, even with the alchemical power of your EMI, takes time. Exploring the archetypal realm and healing polarities can also seem to take forever. However, when your consciousness is centered at the level of intellect/intuition, all time (paradoxically) happens in the eternal now.

The Zen practitioner shares a hopeful slogan, "Before enlightenment, chop wood and carry water. After enlightenment, chop wood and carry water." The key to successfully walking this musical path is to accept yourself and all your permutations right now, not when you have fixed what ails you. To walk this path in the spirit of self-acceptance, patience, curiosity, and positive expectation is to walk with joy. We will explore this joyful state of bliss in the next chapter.

Chapter Seven

Music of Bliss

I felt the sentiment of Being spread
O'er all that moves, and all that seemeth still,
. . . Wonder not
If such my transports were; for in all things now
I saw one life and felt that it was joy.
—William Wordsworth[1]

At the level of intellect/intuition, you harnessed the power of your Essential Musical Intelligence to resolve archetypal core polarities that previously kept you trapped in the grip of ego. In the process of resolving some of these polarities, you inevitably opened to the sublime state of beingness—the wave of serenity that instantly connects you to your essential nature, which is bliss, consciousness, and beauty. In this being state, EMI is constantly singing. Perhaps through your daily practice of music meditation and other depth-oriented musical exercises described in this book, you have similarly entered into the realm beyond the senses and experienced the exquisite silence that yogis call the "unstruck sound" in the cave of the heart. It is here that you will ultimately remember the bliss that is your natural state of being.

The realm of bliss is a center of purity and innocence. Remember Christ's words when he said, "Become as little children and you shall inherit the kingdom of heaven." Bliss is indeed the level of the beginner's mind, free from past and future worries; a state of absolute trust that all your needs are provided for; a place where all fears are dissolved in the harmonizing essence of love.

In a sense, ignorance is bliss. People who do not think and analyze relentlessly seem to be a lot more blissful than people who do. The mind traps us in its ongoing perplexities and while we are in its grip, we are unable to see the larger reality. If you exist in a more instinctual place, connected with your higher self, you are free from the limitations of mind. When you improvise or are deeply immersed in listening to music, you are beyond the mind. That is what EMI is all about. EMI is beyond the thinking realm; rather, it is associated with your ability to surrender to a higher reality and receive your highest good. Thus, once you transcend the limitations of the mind, you instantly connect with the core of your being which is bliss. Music is the key that naturally opens the door.

The Paradoxical Sheath

If the sheaths are like the layers of an onion, bliss is what we get when all the layers have been peeled away. Bliss is there all the time, but we have to remove the sheaths that hide its radiant light. That is why I organized this book using the framework of sheaths. The sheath of intellect/intuition is closest to the level of bliss, but still it blocks the light. The sheath of the mind covers over intellect/intuition, taking us further away from bliss. The sheath of energy/breath covers over the mind, and the sheath of the body masks the energy/breath sheath. The higher up you are in the great chain of being,[2] the closer you come to experiencing bliss. You have to work through the challenges of each level before you can truly manifest, in an ongoing way, this state of bliss in your life.

Paradoxically, although the sheaths are hierarchical levels, they are, at the same time, fluid and permeable, allowing you to experience bliss at any time, even if you haven't completely resolved the challenges of the other sheaths. Transformational work is not linear; it affects your whole being instantaneously. This concept is one of the keynotes of the higher levels of consciousness: once you have transcended mind, all time happens in the eternal now. There are no limitations on how you transform and merge with self. That explains why some people have spontaneous remissions. All the sheaths are pierced with the light of self at same time, and suddenly, for example, the cancer patient has an instantaneous healing. This can be considered a miracle—or just paradox. You don't have to painstakingly resolve every little problem that gets in the way of higher consciousness, but at the same time you have to do the work.

In other words, healing is not necessarily magic, but it can be. That is the nature of paradox—the mystery of what can happen when you go beyond the mind. As you can see now, your Essential Musical Intelligence is like a river that flows through every sheath, patiently awaiting your command for integration to occur on all levels. Its ultimate goal is to lead you back to the source, the eternal ocean of bliss.

Channeling the Music of Bliss

Bliss is akin to artistic rapture, the feeling that you, the artist, are not merely playing music, but are being used as a vessel for the expression of archetypal information from a higher source. Artistic rapture is related to channeling, the ability to set aside the thinking mind in order to receive messages from the higher self and share them with others through the creative process.

For example, when I improvise at the piano, I sometimes enter a state of rapture in which I find myself playing strange rhythms and otherworldly harmonies that are foreign to my nature. My dogs, who are probably my most devoted fans, usually respond to this change in consciousness by pricking their ears and looking around as if they sense another presence. For as long as the music lasts, they are mesmerized.

In these moments of connecting with a higher force, we are truly channeling some deeper reality or archetypal energy. Some animals—particularly dogs and cats—can sense that, because they are naturally more attuned to sound and vibration than humans. I perceive the information that flows through me during these ecstatic sojourns as a gift that enhances my ability to communicate musically with others and to understand the musical gifts received by others. Channeling allows me to feel that I am part of something much larger, more powerful, and more radiant than I can ever be—and yet, paradoxically, it *is* me.

Natural Bliss

Places in nature can evoke the experience of bliss. For me, Big Sur, along the central California coast, is such a place. The seemingly endless miles of raw beauty—mountains, ocean, forest, sky—all blend into one delicious gestalt. There is serenity wherever you look. The first time I visited Big Sur, I asked my friend, a native Californian, where the town was. She replied that there wasn't a town. In fact, there was no *there* there. This, for me, was the epitome of the bliss realm. There is nowhere to go because you are already there. Similarly, bliss is not something to achieve tomorrow. You can have it now, in this moment. You don't have to work for bliss; you can celebrate your essential self right here, right now, and music is the perfect venue. By tuning into EMI you can be totally present and fully *experience* the moment, as opposed to obsessing over the past or worrying about the future.

Techniques for Attaining the State of Bliss

Bliss comes to us in moments of silence. Most of us never seriously consider the benefits of being silent. Within the yoga tradition, however, the ability to achieve inner silence is a necessary step for enlightenment. In my early days of meditation practice and healing with music and sound, I asked my meditation teacher to instruct me in *nada* yoga (the science of sound). I expected years of difficult mantras and yantras and impossible yoga postures. Nevertheless, I felt ready to move to the next level. To my great surprise (and relief), my teacher instructed me to find a very quiet place in nature where I was to merely listen. In this place, he explained, all would be revealed. "Is that it?" I thought. "Just sit and be quiet?" Sitting still for long periods of time was a tall order for a hyper New Yorker like me. My teacher suggested that I spend a couple of days in seclusion, just being with myself, not speaking to anyone, not reading anything secular or exposing myself to anything that required ego-based thinking or planning. I was asked to create a time for self-reflection, a time to experience myself from moment to moment, a time to sink into the silence.

My teacher's request reminded me of the exquisite silence that my friend Bob and I had experienced years before during an extraordinary camping trip in the Sangre de Cristo Mountains of southern Colorado, just as winter's frost was beginning to thaw. It was spring break, and Bob and I, then students at UC Boulder, decided to visit an alternative school of *higher* learning—about ten thousand feet above sea level! With enough clothes and supplies for a week, we arrived at a well-hidden mountain trail and hiked five miles deep into the woods. There we came to a clearing where Bob had erected two large teepees on private family-owned land, one for sleeping and cooking, the other for storage. There was no one around for miles and miles. We were completely isolated; there wasn't even a national park in the vicinity.

After about two days of being completely alone in nature and thoroughly immersed in every aspect of the five elements—earth, sun, the pristine mountain air, nourishing water from the mountain streams, organic food, radiant stars at night—we found that we couldn't speak. There was simply nothing to say. We both lapsed into altered states of complete serenity. Soon everything we did was blissful: just pouring bottled water into a metal cup and drinking it was an amazing experience.

Five days later, it was time to go home. During our six-hour drive back to Boulder, we still did not utter a word. There was just a glow between us. When I got back to my apartment, my roommate greeted me, but still I couldn't speak. I glanced at myself in the bathroom mirror and noticed that my appearance was remarkably different. There were no lines of worry on my face; I looked as pure and innocent as a baby. It took about two days before I started to speak again, and even then, I had to push through my desire *not* to speak. For an urban girl who had never enjoyed any private space growing up, I soon realized that there was more to life than just talking, doing, collecting, and achieving. I knew I would never be quite the same.

I had forgotten about that experience until my teacher brought up the idea of consciously planning my own silence retreat. I hope that you too will allow yourself to know this kind of bliss.

Practicing silence involves a commitment of time during which you do not talk, read, or think and plan about anything related to your day-to-day life. It is a time for introspection and contemplation of your reason for being in the world, to become a witness to your inner life, to learn to be fully present in your body, and to sink into the reality of who you truly are. I suggest that you take a vow stating when you will start and end your silence and put it in writing. Plan your retreat for a time when you will not be disturbed or tempted to change your mind. You might start with one full day, and later, three days, then five. An ideal place for a silence retreat is an ashram or retreat center where a beautiful, peaceful environment will make the experience more inviting.

Silence Retreat

Our noisy years seem moments in
the being of the eternal silence.
—William Wordsworth

Bring your Music and Sound Awareness Journal with you and take the time to record insights, feelings, and revelations that arise from your deeper self. Other than that, avoid all activity except walking meditation, contemplation of the five elements, listening within, engaging your EMI, and the necessities of eating, sleeping, bathing, and daily spiritual practices. Note at the end of your first day any changes in feelings, energy states, thought patterns, and bodily sensations. No doubt you will experience some wonderful results.

The practice of silence is not easy. Most of us are addicted to filling the space around us with magazines and newspapers, hours of television and movies, and surfing the worldwide web until the wee hours. Mass media are a great distraction to our ability to achieve serenity. In addition, many of us do not feel alive if we don't constantly give and receive feedback from others throughout the day.

With this relentless stream of incoming data filling your psychic space, silence may actually be a shock to your system! Many people experience varying degrees of anxiety when they find themselves alone in the creative void. This is a perfect time to tune into Essential Musical Intelligence. Take the witness stance and watch your fears as opposed to identifying with them and letting them control your behavior. Once you have created some distance from them, you can activate your discriminative capacity and let go of irrational, inefficient thoughts and feelings. Another way to deal with anxiety is to embrace the fear musically through improvisation. With practice, you will be able to sink into the silence and allow its sweetness to fill you with indescribable joy.

Chanting the Road To Bliss

In the beginning was the word, and the word was God.
The Word whistled through the reeds,
sang through the trees, and swirled through the chasms of space.
In imitation of this sound, man formed the vowels,
and, according to the Kabala, therein found the name of God.
—Anonymous

Another way to penetrate the sheaths and enter into bliss is through chanting. From time immemorial, people the world over have chanted as a way to worship and call upon the Divine. In most spiritual traditions, the words and sounds that make up chants are typically seed mantras, or words of power, that can be perceived as direct manifestations of divine consciousness. When we chant, the rhythmical repetition of the musical phrase leads the mind into an altered state of consciousness. Here we may become one with the universal truths expressed through the chant that allows us the experience of immeasurable joy.

The secret to the achievement of bliss through chanting is surrender to the universal pulse inherent in your natural breath rhythms (being), as opposed to singing on the beat (doing). In this state of mind, you *let* the chant happen through you, rather than *make* it happen. When you are connected to the universal pulse, all your natural rhythms fall in sync to create a sense of internal coherence, which leads to clarity, harmony, and ecstasy. You will know when you have made this connection because your body will begin on its own accord to move with the pulse. This activation of core spinal energies often leads to cathartic movement and emotional release which in themselves can be ecstatic.

Chants from various spiritual traditions can lead you to a blissful state. The following are some of my favorites. You can sing them as a prelude to meditation or yoga or any time you need a bliss break. If you prefer chanting with others, join an ongoing yoga society that has regular *kirtans* (chanting sessions), or start your own chanting group. It's inevitable: the more you sing the chants that are most meaningful to you, the more blissful you become.

The first chants I practiced were those recommended by Western mystic Edgar Cayce.

YA HE VA HE – (YAH hay VAH hay) Cayce translates these syllables as the ability to know your own uniqueness and, at the same time, your oneness with the infinite.

ARE RE OM – (AH-ray ohm) This chant is intoned on a single note over the course of one exhalation. It assists you in drawing in the love of the Absolute Being.[3]

The chants that follow are well-known traditional chants from several spiritual traditions. I suggest that you choose one and work with it for a couple of weeks or months (or years!) so that its meaning can gradually be absorbed and integrated into the fabric of your unconscious mind. The more you practice your chosen chant, the more you will experience its harmonizing, healing influence in all areas of your life.

NAM MYOHO RENGE KYO - (nahm mee-YO-ho REN-gay KEE-yo) A Japanese chant repeated rapidly on one tone over period of ten minutes or more, this chant is a major practice of Nichiren Shoshu Buddhism. It is dedicated to the ultimate law of cause and effect through sound. Aspirants repeat these words at their altars each morning and evening and at other times as needed for centering.

OM NAMAHA SHIVAYA – (ohm nah-MAH-hah shih-VIE-ah) A widely chanted Sanskrit mantra to Shiva. It can be translated as "I honor the Divine within."

LA ILAHA ILLALLAH HU – (la il-LA-ha il-LA-lah-ah-HU) A traditional Sufi chant that means "there is no God but God." Traditionally, this chant is sung during *zhikrs* (ceremonies of remembrance). The chant is intoned slowly at first on a single pitch, while the head circles to the right and up (LA ILAHA), then down to the left (IL LALLAH HU). This gesture is said to "put God in the heart."

Longtime chanting advocate Robbie Gass quotes Sufi Murshid Elias Amidon in his description of zhikr: "Remembering who we are, remembering God, and bringing the Divine into our consciousness through music."[4] To me, this is also a perfect definition of Essential Musical Intelligence.

OM TARE TUTARE TURE SVAHA – (ohm TA-rah TOO-tah-rah TOO-ray svah-ha) A Green Tara (Buddhist) mantra that helps you develop compassion for all you meet, irrespective of their position in life. This mantra is sung in rounds of 108 times and is said to end suffering in the lives of those who chant it.

LISTEN, LISTEN, LISTEN – A great devotional chant by Paramahansa Yogananda.

Listen, listen, listen to my heart's song.
Listen, listen, listen to my heart's song.
I will never forget you, I will never forsake you.
Never forget you, I will never forsake you.
Listen, listen, listen to my heart's song.[5]

ALLELUIA – (AH-lay-LOO-yah) Means "Praise the Lord." It can be arranged in four-part harmony to the melody of Pachelbel's Canon.

GATE GATE PARA GATE PARA SAM GATE, BODHI SVAHA – (GAH-tay GAH-tay PAH-rah GAH-tay PAH-rah SAHM gah-TAY, BOH-dee SVAH-hah) This chant embodies the Buddha's teachings on the illusory nature of reality and the path to awakening from suffering. It means: "Gone. Gone. Gone beyond. Gone beyond the beyond."

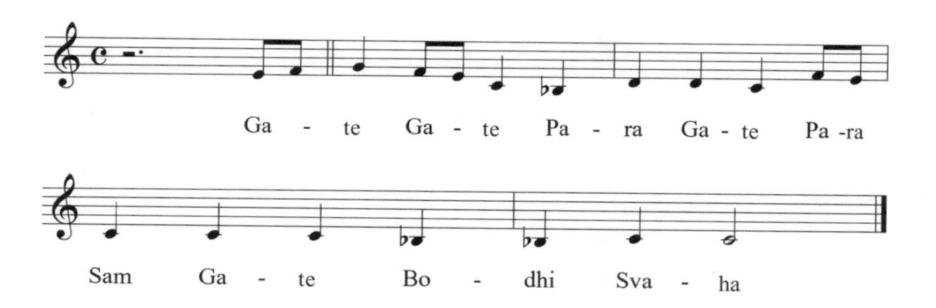

Overtone Producing

One of the secrets of entering the state of bliss while chanting is the production of overtones. Overtones are a series of barely audible higher-pitched tones that originate from a single fundamental tone. When resonated together with the fundamental tone, they create a harmony. Overtones give specific musical instruments their distinct sound and color. Overtones are also produced while singing and are most easily heard when we chant. Whenever we resonate a tone, there is the potential to create one or two additional higher-pitched overtones at the same time, depending on which vowel sound we hold and how our vocal palates are shaped. These higher tones speak directly to the core of our being, reminding us of the essential harmony that exists both within us and without. Although quite subtle, you can hear and feel the effect of overtones while listening to recordings of Mongolian overtone chanting, ritual chanting of the Gyuto Tantric Monks, traditional Gregorian chants, Sufi chants, and the more secular chants of David Hykes and the Harmonic Choir. You will experience the most profound effects while practicing them yourself.

The overtone series (also known as the harmonic series) was first discovered by Pythagoras in his experiments with the monochord (a single-stringed instrument) in 700 BCE. Pythagoras determined that a string vibrates not only as a whole, but also in segments of halves, thirds, fourths, fifths, sevenths, eighths, and so on, up to sixteenths. He also discovered that each segment vibrated in exactly the same manner as the whole, but at a faster rate than the fundamental pitch.

For example, the first overtone has a frequency twice the rate of the fundamental tone; the second overtone has a frequency three times the frequency of the fundamental; the third overtone's frequency is four times, and so on. Our Western musical scale was derived from the musical ratios of the overtone series. For example, 1:1 represents the fundamental. The ratio 1:2 creates an octave. Similarly, 2:3 is a fifth, 3:4 the interval of a fourth, and 4:5 the interval of a major third. There are an infinite number of overtones that sound along with each fundamental note. As we move higher up in the series, the intervals become smaller and the overtones surpass our audible limits (20–20,000 hertz). Thus, a great proportion of the overtones travel in silence, as subliminal sound.

The Harmonic Series

The whole-tone relationships that make up the harmonic series can be found throughout the natural world. For example, the exact harmonic proportions of the octave, fifth, fourth, etc. are found in the structure of the human body, in the planetary orbits, and in the way leaves are spaced on a tree branch. These mathematical relationships are also reflected in the sacred architecture of certain monuments, cathedrals, and pyramids. The absolutely predictable repetition of the harmonic series in all aspects of life on our planet suggests that music is the fundamental building block of creation. Viewed from the level of bliss, this musical harmony represents the innate perfection at the core of life.

You can harmonize your body, mind, and spirit through overtone chanting. To be able to sing overtones, you have to train your ear and voice so that you can hear and then isolate specific sounds above a fundamental tone while you are chanting. Once you have mastered the technique, you can then surrender to the sublime fullness of the sound.

Overtone Chanting

You may practice this exercise either lying down or sitting up with head, neck, and trunk aligned. Begin by relaxing your mind-body and practicing diaphragmatic breathing. Then warm up your voice by toning for several minutes.

Hum an MMM sound using the deepest, lowest tone that you can muster without strain. From the MMM sound, gradually shift to a slightly more open MO sound. Now open a bit more to an AH sound. Allow the sound to move deeper into the throat with a long I (like the word *eye*) sound and, finally, further back in the throat with an EE sound. In one sweep of breath, the overtone exercise should sound like this: MMM-MO-AH-I-EE. Listen for the tiny overtones floating on top of your fundamental tone with each shifting phoneme. Make sure that you breathe diaphragmatically and that the sound comes from your belly. This allows the overtones to be more pronounced. See if you can actually isolate the most prominent overtones (octave, fifth, major third, dominant seventh) and play with their intensity. With time, you may even be able to create little melodies with the overtones above the fundamental tone. Practice for five to ten minutes. When you are finished, lie down and rest.[6]

At first, overtone chanting is best practiced in a resonant space, preferably near water. When I first started to practice, I would lie in my bathtub and sing overtones. It was much easier for me to hear them in the cavelike acoustics of my bathroom than anyplace else. It was also calming after a long day of work. An excellent way to develop your listening skills so that you can actually hear and discriminate overtones is meditating on the sounds of waterfalls. There are so many layers of sound and rhythm resonating from a waterfall. With practice you will be able to discriminate between all the different parts that create the harmonic roar of your favorite waterfall. Training your ear to discriminate these sounds and rhythms inevitably hones your ability to listen more carefully and deeply and expands your own personal roar while making music.

Overtone chanting not only leads to bliss, it also creates balance, order, and a laserlike focus. Only when the mind is focused and stilled can it be transcended. In addition, overtone chanting can be salutary to your health. French neurologist Alfred Tomatis discovered that certain high-frequency sounds energize or charge the nervous system.[7] This finding suggests that when you feel tired or worn out, an infusion of the high-frequency sounds associated with overtone chanting can stimulate your creative juices. Tomatis' theory also implies that it is possible to use overtone chanting as a healing modality. The intensive listening required to produce overtones may activate the muscles of the inner ear associated with focusing and integration. As listening and attention are honed from the inside out, you can better cope with a variety of mind-body problems, including depression, learning disabilities, and some neurological disorders.

Chanting as a Group

The effects of overtone chanting can be most powerfully felt when performed in a group of at least four individuals. The more people there are chanting together, the more the overtones are magnified, creating what we might imagine as the sound of an angelic choir. This kind of chanting subtly breaks down boundaries between individuals, leading to increased feelings of serenity, joy, and oneness.

Group Harmonic Chanting

Harmonic chanting can be used prior to a healing service as a way to attune group members, or it can be used simply as a deeply calming, centering exercise to facilitate bliss and unity among a group of individuals. Start by forming a circle with participants sitting either on chairs or floor cushions. The designated leader begins with an invocation, stating the purpose of the group (healing, world peace, inner travel) and requesting the power of Absolute Being to assist in the process. During the invocation, it is quite beneficial for the participants to awaken their Essential Musical Intelligence by softly playing small gongs or Tibetan or crystal bell bowls, bamboo or wooden flutes, or other meditative instruments. Once the group is attuned and deeply relaxed, the leader begins the chant by intoning a note that is then immediately mirrored and held lovingly by the group. While intoning the fundamental note, the group gradually begins to experiment with different overtones. It is best to stay with the same fundamental tone for a while until the group becomes cohesive. Once the group is in sync, individuals can move from the fundamental tone and sing harmony parts while continuing to create overtones.

As the chanting becomes more harmonic, the group naturally begins to weave together tapestries of sound with a fullness that is seldom matched in large choirs. Individual chanters typically report feeling waves of energy moving through them as they sing;

some experience vibrant imagery or intense emotions; occasionally spontaneous healing and cathartic movement occur in one or more members. Group overtone chanting creates a tangible experience of wholeness (what mystic Dane Rudhyar called the *pleroma*) that is irresistible. One chanter described it as the sublime feeling of being lovingly held in an ocean of sound.

The music of group harmonic chanting usually moves in a wavelike format. The chanting ebbs and flows for a period of time (usually between twenty and forty-five minutes) until magically the entire group stops at once. Each member then sinks into a deep, full silence that envelops the entire group. It is almost impossible to speak afterward. Many naturally fall into deep meditation. The effects of chanting usually last for several hours and seem to have a cumulative positive effect.

In utilizing harmonic chanting for healing purposes, ask the patient to lie in the middle of the circle of chanters and allow the sound to cleanse the etheric body and induce healing imagery. The patient can also be encouraged to make sounds (along with the chanters) to give voice to unexpressed emotions, memories, and fantasies associated with his or her illness.

Trance, Ritual, and EMI

Another way of entering bliss is through musical trance induction. Music, chanting, drumming, and repetitive movement that stimulate core spinal energies are used to facilitate trance in healing rituals all over the world, especially in shamanic cultures and the major spiritual traditions of both East and West. Participants chant specific songs or mantras to invoke Absolute Being or the power of nature to manifest what is needed for an individual or group. Ceremonial drumming and repetitive movements that directly stimulate core spinal energies are also included in all trance-inducing rituals. The combination of chanting, drumming, and movement (whirling or hopping) carried out over a long period of time helps participants enter altered states of consciousness where they may access the archetypal realms for self-exploration and healing.

Following are a couple of personal stories that demonstrate the power of trance in activating the bliss state.

Shamanic Tradition

Several years ago while I was teaching a workshop on music and healing in Seoul, Korea, I was invited by my colleague, Dr. Jinsook Kim, to pay a visit to a traditional shaman village. Jinsook explained to me that every weekend, scores of people flock to the village, located in the lush green mountains outside the city, to seek cures for a variety of ills that cannot be healed by Western medicine. The village is made up of huts and ceremonial altars where shamans perform their healing rituals. In her doctoral studies on Korean shamanism, Jinsook found that improvised music and song are integral components of all the healing rituals in this village. In fact, according to Jinsook, without the ritual music and dance at the start of each ceremony, the shamans cannot enter the trance state.

On the morning of our visit, Jinsook and I decided to first take a hike in the hills surrounding the village in order to ground and center ourselves. As we walked deeper into the woods, we began to hear strains of otherworldly music. We hiked in the direction of the sounds, which soon led us to a small campsite. There we found a young Korean shaman dressed in blue silk pajamas, sitting erect, yet deep in trance, chanting and creating hypnotic sounds and rhythms on a small drum and an array of gongs and bells. We were mesmerized. We sat for what seemed like hours, falling into trance ourselves, until the shaman tapped us on our shoulders and graciously invited us into his lean-to for tea. As we emerged from our trance states, we felt remarkably refreshed and clear headed.

The musician told us that his name was Jungso and that he had been living alone in the mountains for several months. Jungso explained that his master (a renowned Korean shaman) had sent him to entertain the Mountain Spirit (guardian of the village) for 100 days and nights so that the spirit would bring good fortune to all who sought his assistance. Jungso radiated an aura of contagious joy and exuberance as he spoke. Even though I could not understand the language, I felt quite connected to both Jungso and Jinsook and joined them in sharing several moments of deep contentment and bliss.

Later that evening, after returning to my hotel room in Seoul, I reflected on the music of the day. I still felt a warm glow within and wondered what had really been expressed through Jungso's music. It soon became clear that the young shaman, first, in surrendering his will to that of his master and second, by immersing himself deeply in musical improvisation as both worship and praise of higher being, had truly transcended the limitations of his ego. He had entered into the realm of bliss through his own ritual and trance induction and naturally had become a clear, potent channel for EMI.

Spiritual Tradition

The most profound experience of bliss that I have encountered to date was at an intensive retreat several years ago with Sufi master Adnan Sarhan in New York City. About fifty aspirants had committed to a week of total immersion in Sufi spiritual practices. After hours of intense yogalike physical exercises, chanting, and drumming during the first day of the retreat, we were ready to engage in the sacred ritual of remembering, called *zhikr*. During the zhikr, all of us, seated on the floor in cross-legged positions, were led by Adnan in chanting, *La ilaha illalah hu* ("There is no God but God") while moving our heads in a circular fashion to the rhythm of the words. The chanting, accompanied by Turkish musicians who created a rhythmic drone on large frame drums, started out slowly. After about ten minutes of relaxed, yet rigorous chanting, I began to fall in and out of consciousness. It was as if my mind had been loosed from my body and hung out to air . . . so freeing!

After a while, the chanting and drumming increased in tempo. The intensity of the music began to pull me into an even deeper trance state. I was determined to resist its pull, however, and tried to remain conscious and continue chanting with the group. At one point, however, I just let go. All at once, waves of indescribable joy began to envelop me. I had never experienced anything like it: I had become one with the infinite sea of bliss.

After another twenty minutes, Adnan began to slow the pulse of the music. At that point, my body had disappeared, my emotions had disappeared, and my mind was nowhere to be found. I simply felt myself as pure being. I was unable to move. It seemed like I had sat in that place of being for a very long while. When it finally came time to leave, I practically floated home, still in a state of bliss. The sensation lasted for several hours and left a deep impression. I realized that this experience of bliss was a call to remembrance of my true nature. And this remembrance—the source of my Essential Musical Intelligence—has enabled me to move forward with confidence on my rainbow journey.

Similarly, in more secular settings, people long for the experience of trance where they can let go completely and merge with others while being held in the loving arms of Mother Muse. You may have had this kind of experience while listening to certain rock groups that engaged in jams where the musicians improvised chorus after chorus, building the intensity of the music to the level of wild abandon (the Grateful Dead or Santana); or at a free-jazz concert where you became entrained by the sounds and rhythms of virtuoso improvisers and jazz innovators like John Coltrane, Cecil Taylor, and Ornette Coleman. Or perhaps you have engaged in a more contemporary practice of musical trance induction—the rave. Here scores of people, in an effort to escape the constraints of mind, gather in huge public spaces with psychedelic lights flashing and dance to the likes of Techno/Indian raga music for hours until they reach the state of bliss they so desperately seek.

Even the business world is not immune to the effects of trance-inducing ritual. A number of major corporations now sponsor regular drumming circles as a stress-reducing employee benefit. Here once buttoned-down executives collectively express their passion and angst through drumming, howling, and ecstatic movement, and are born again in the creative unfolding of their Essential Musical Intelligence.

All of the above rituals begin with a repetitive, rhythm-based musical activity that creates a secure framework for aspirants to travel inward, followed by some kind of spontaneous musical expression that allows them to experience what they need in order to become more whole. Again we witness the elegant process of engaging EMI.

CHAPTER SEVEN

Mysticism, EMJ, and the Path of the Heart

Mystics seek to transcend the constraints of the ego and live exclusively in the bliss realm. Through their relentless quest to resolve polarities in the archetypal realm, they strive toward the suspension of dualism to become supra-individual witnesses capable of observing the flow of what is without manipulating it. Mystics blaze a trail for the rest of us so that we can move with a certain degree of confidence toward the light. Spiritual teachers, transcendental poets, painters, composers, healers, and others who have surrendered their will to that of Absolute Being all have a mystical attunement. Having opened their higher chakras (heart, throat, third eye, and crown) through devotion to truth and obedience to an inner calling, they may become direct channels for higher wisdom.

Because higher wisdom comes from the realm beyond mind, it is most often transmitted through the language of paradox, which reflects the wisdom of the heart. For example, take a few moments to reflect on the following words of Ramon Llull, the great medieval spiritual thinker and poet of the Island of Majorca: "Love is that which places the free in bondage and to those in bondage gives freedom."[8]

It may take a while for its meaning to sink in, but when it does we experience a kind of "Aha!" moment, an awakening of heart intelligence. Paradox is also reflected in music where, for instance, two contradictory themes or emotions are expressed at the same time, yet they create a harmony that can be perceived only by a higher faculty. The music of romantic composer Ludwig von Beethoven often reflects this phenomenon. In the inscription to his transcendental work, the *Missa Solemnis,* Beethoven wrote, "From the heart it comes, to the heart is must go." Take some time to listen to this masterpiece. Where does the music take you?

Many mystics follow what the yogis call the Bhakti path, or path of the heart, also described as "loving self-forgetfulness in service of the God known to yourself." Jesus, for example, expressed this concept in his cryptic statement, "I and my Father are one." Through communion with Absolute Being, mystics make significant contributions to humanity because they are filled and nurtured by divinity. As channels of higher wisdom, mystics give people what they need as opposed to what they want; they speak the truth. Consequently, many have been ostracized and even persecuted because their views did not reflect the status quo. Suffering, however, does not hinder the mystically inclined on their journey. They live in the world, yet remain unattached. Thus, mystics experience the bliss that comes with freedom. They have completely embodied step two of the transformational process of engaging EMI. Mystics know through and through that they are God's perfect children and that harmony rules in their universe.

Love: the Music of Bliss

Listen far beyond hearing,
and call the unheard.
—Lao Tzu

As you continue practicing the exercises presented in this book, your heart will become more open to the music of bliss and you will ultimately realize that love is the only true power there is. Perhaps you have already discovered that love is the living breath of the soul, and EMI its audible expression. In embracing this reality, you too will walk the path of the mystic. Once on this path, you will release all prior ways of knowing about self and the world and listen from an impersonal perspective.[9] Only then can you listen with a beginner's mind that seeks no solution, has no need to repair or fix, grasps no ideas or concepts, and is simply present in loving openness.

I would like to share with you a powerful technique to move your consciousness out of the limitations of the ego and into a more heart-centered, impersonal stance, which I call the Giving-and-Receiving Feedback Loop. This deceptively simple exercise, practiced diligently, can be one of the best catalysts for self-transformation. It starts with the assumption that we reap what we sow. By giving selflessly and unconditionally, we naturally receive abundance in our lives. When we hold back because of fear or doubt, we put up barriers that block our potential abundance. It is important to remember, however, that giving is not about *shoulds*. As I said earlier, the mystic gives people what they need, not necessarily what they want. The gift comes from an impersonal place of heart knowing, not from mental constructs. But how do we know what people need? This exercise will help you develop your inner listening capacity, your ability to sense the deeper needs of others, and to use your EMI to give them what is needed. It is best to practice this exercise with a partner, although you can use it to connect with someone at a distance.

Giving-and-Receiving Feedback Loop

Gather some of your improvisation instruments and sit facing your partner at a comfortable distance. Both of you should relax and clear yourselves with the Breath Awareness exercise. Now begin breathing in and out through your heart center. Allow yourself to become so quiet that you can almost hear your heart beating. Visualize a golden light radiating from the center of your chest. See it growing larger, creating a field in and around you and your partner.

Now tune into the energy of your partner. Enter into the impersonal stance by letting the boundaries between the two of you soften. Imagine that you can actually become your partner for a moment. This is a way of relating deeply, yet impersonally. Once you get a sense of your partner's being, give your partner a gift of improvised music (either vocal, instrumental, or both). You may first want to go through the steps of activating your EMI, or just let your musical gift unfold naturally. Play for as long as the energy moves you. Then sit quietly and feel the effects of the interaction.

If you are the receiver in this exercise, you are asked to receive your partner's musical gift unconditionally. If thoughts, judgments, or resistance arise, it is important to let them go and focus from the heart center on receiving your partner's gift.

As your partner opens to receive your gift, she allows more of her truth to be revealed. As her true self becomes more accessible, you send out even more love and healing energy through your music. Your partner responds with an increased capacity to receive your communication. This allows you more space to give; thus, the Giving-and-Receiving Feedback Loop is activated. Neither giver nor receiver thinks about what is going on; both of you are in a state beyond mind, one of receptivity and surrender associated with the bliss state where miracles can happen.

It is often difficult to talk about this once it is over, because the interaction between you and your partner takes place at the soul level, which is expressed through music, sound, and image. In addition, ego-oriented boundaries are loosened and you experience a sense of oneness just being together in the music. Thus, at its deepest level, the Giving-and-Receiving Feedback Loop dissolves all separation between you and your partner. While resonating together through the musical exchange, you are united in the spirit of love and unconditional acceptance. The more you practice this exercise, particularly with individuals or groups that you dislike or judge, the more you will develop the ability to interact impersonally. In this state, music heals both you and others.

I developed the feedback-loop technique while conducting a stress-management workshop for musicians who suffered extreme performance anxiety. These people had a terrible time with auditions and juries because they perceived their evaluators as unforgiving critics who were out to get them. Because they went through their auditions with such a defensive mindset, they forfeited the possibility of experiencing joy and giving love and comfort through their music.

I pointed out to the students that evaluators are just people doing their jobs. They have issues and hang-ups just like anyone else. Musicians tend to idealize their evaluators and imbue them with the power to make or break them. I asked Ann, a particularly anxious classical pianist, to describe the personalities of the raters on her last jury. She took great delight in describing one pianist/rater as bored and filled with disdain. Another she characterized as "wound up too tight"—very rigid. Ann described the third rater as grandiose and self-involved. The fourth was actually her own piano teacher. Ann depicted her as meek, a real people pleaser.

Then I asked Ann to choose individuals among the workshop participants to play the role of each rater. To her surprise, she easily found doubles for each one. The "raters" were then asked to improvise music appropriate to their unique personalities. It is uncanny how, when listening with the ear of the heart, we know exactly what the music of others sounds like. Ann was blown away by the accuracy of the doubles' spontaneous musical expression. I then asked Ann to activate the Giving-and-Receiving Feedback Loop and to play with each rater individually, to tune into each, take on the impersonal stance, and give to each what he or she needed—not what Ann thought they might want to hear.

What Ann discovered was that each rater needed love and healing. Her heart-felt improvisations transformed the pain and resistance expressed by the raters and created a mutual environment of calm acceptance and reverence. Ann later told me that now, whenever she has an audition or jury, she first activates the Giving-and-Receiving Feedback Loop and gives her music with love. This practice has almost completely neutralized her performance anxiety.

Healing and the Giving-and-Receiving Feedback Loop

You can use the Giving-and-Receiving Feedback Loop to create harmony in an existing, past, or nascent relationship; to transform and integrate uncooperative subpersonalities; or to connect deeply with someone and assist him or her in being and becoming, either face-to-face or at a distance. The following story demonstrates how this may be done.

While I was working as a music therapist at Memorial Sloan

Kettering, a cancer hospital in New York City, I was asked to visit a sixty-three-year-old terminally ill woman whom doctors had described as severely depressed, hostile, and "living on borrowed time." The head nurse explained that Jean's body had been deteriorating for some time due to the ravages of end-stage multiple sclerosis and metastatic lung cancer. Jean constantly complained that she wanted to die, that she had had enough, but for some reason she remained stuck in what she called her "unrelenting limbo state."

When I arrived with my musical instruments in tow at Jean's room, she was alone and seemed glad to see me. I was surprised to find that such a sick woman could still have a gleam in her eye. I told her a little bit about myself and about my work. Jean told me about her family (two sons, a daughter, and a doting husband) and her history of devastating illnesses. Jean's husband, her constant companion, had just been hospitalized with a mild heart attack, and this was the first time she could remember being without him. She explained that his absence had given her some time to think. Although Jean appeared too weak to make music at the moment, I felt compelled to know her better.

After a lull in our conversation, I asked Jean if she had any regrets, if there was something she had always wanted to do but had never gotten around to. To my surprise, she said that she had always wanted to be a jazz singer. As a young woman, she had sung in clubs, and those experiences were her most memorable. Once she got married, however, her husband forbade her to sing; he didn't want other men to desire her. So she hid her passion and became a dutiful wife. Right around the time she stopped singing, she developed multiple sclerosis. She soon became totally dependent on her husband's care. He relished his caretaker role and took an early retirement so that he could devote all his time to her.

I asked Jean if she had a favorite song that she used to sing, and she quickly replied, "East of the Sun (and West of the Moon)," by Brooks Bowman. I wasn't familiar with the tune, so I asked Jean if she could sing it. A warm smile radiated from her gaunt yet beautiful face. "I can't sing," she replied. "I am sure that you can," I insisted. "I would really love to hear it." She looked around the room as if to make sure that no one else would hear, and then, in a subdued yet sexy voice, began to sing, "East of the sun, and west of the moon. We'll build a dream house of love, dear . . ."

Tears welled up in my eyes as I imagined Jean in her prime, feeling her passion, expressing her gift. I grabbed my portable keyboard and accompanied her as best I could. The music really swung and Jean was remarkably alive. After singing the first verse, she stopped and became still, as if listening to some inner music, her smile still beaming. "That's enough," she said. "I am tired now." She looked at me and asked, "Will you remember me in your prayers tonight?" I told her that I would.

Later that evening while improvising at my piano, I remembered Jean's request. I decided to activate the Giving-and-Receiving Feedback Loop. I closed my eyes and visualized Jean in her hospital bed. I called upon my EMI and focused on sending a musical gift from my heart to hers. The improvisation was intense. It expressed waves of pure passion, sensuality, and aggression mixed with tenderness. I felt like I was literally connecting with Jean and that we were engaged in a dialogue that drew from our depths. I intuitively knew that I was receiving her inner music, which fueled the fire in mine. The music lasted for about fifteen minutes. When it was over, I knew that something important had occurred. I felt a deep sensation of peace, a quiet resolution. I knew that Jean felt it too.

I looked forward to checking in with Jean the following day. When I arrived at her room the next morning, I found that her bed had been stripped. I felt a lump in my throat. Jean's nurse appeared in the doorway and told me that Jean had passed away peacefully during the night. She was finally freed from her unrelenting limbo. I couldn't speak for several minutes. Instead, I began to hear fragments of last night's improvisation and the haunting lyrics of Jean's favorite song: "Up among the stars we'll find a harmony of life to a lovely tune . . ."

You have now come full circle in awakening your Essential Musical Intelligence and using it to explore and transform each level of consciousness. This creative musical process will lead you to your final goal of self-realization. However, it is important to acknowledge that roadblocks may emerge along the way to prevent you from connecting with EMI when you most need to. Many of these roadblocks are related to unresolved early trauma, which can cause developmental arrest or fragmentation of the self, resulting in the creation of subpersonalities that may or not be in harmony with your true self.[10] In the following chapter we will focus on the music of trauma.

Chapter Eight

Music of Trauma

Truly,
it is in the darkness that one finds the light,
so when we are in sorrow,
then this light is nearest of all to us.
—Meister Eckhart

Essential Musical Intelligence is the voice of your true self. When you are centered and secure in your identity as a valuable, creative human being, its expression is unimpeded. Unfortunately, not all people resonate with this ideal reality. If, during your precious developmental years, you were harshly criticized, abandoned, parentified (made to act like an adult way before you were ready to do so), or psychically annihilated through overwhelming physical, emotional, or sexual abuse, you probably found ways of creating a false self and/or dissociating from your core being in order to protect yourself from additional pain. When you are disconnected from your core self or living out your reality in the grip of an undeveloped or fearful subpersonality, it is difficult to acknowledge your Essential Musical Intelligence. Emotional, mental, and physical trauma affect your sense of trust in the inherent goodness of yourself and of the world at large. Step 2 of the process of engaging your Essential Musical Intelligence depends upon your ability to remember your divine worth.

Most people who experienced early trauma subsequently believe that the abuse was their fault, that they are defective and qualitatively different from others, and that they are unworthy of love and abundance. When they receive good things, they often feel guilt or shame. Thus, it is difficult for people with unresolved trauma to tread confidently on the path of EMI. The process of activating EMI could bring up intense feelings of doubt, guilt, shame, and despair, which obviously conflict with the more positive experiences that connecting with essential creativity can bring.

When it is not safe to be who you are because of the threat of abuse or abandonment, the ego fragments as a way of protecting the core self from being destroyed.[1] These fragments are either dissociated and hidden from the self and can be realized only when experiences similar to the original trauma occur; or they may develop into subpersonalities that influence the flow of your daily life. Subpersonalities have qualitatively unique identities. For example, one might reflect the moods, desires, and temperament of your internalized mother; another, of your father; and yet another, of your abused inner child. With severe trauma, the abused child subpersonality is frozen at the age when the primary trauma occurred. When this subpersonality dominates, it can wreak havoc with your adult goals and desires. Of course, the core self is always present at some level. Depending on the amount of fragmentation, however, its presence is often overshadowed by the unfulfilled desires and needs of conflicting subpersonalities.[2]

It takes a lot of psychic energy to deal with these conflicting ego states. Ideally, this same energy could be used more productively in facilitating creative growth and change, but instead, the subpersonalities, which are typically fear based, resist change and keep you centered in survival mode. As the song says, however, "You can't please everyone (subpersonalities), so you've got to please yourself (core self)." The way to harmonize and integrate these fragments into a whole is to first become aware of who they are and when they are throwing you off balance; and second, to find a way for your core self to lovingly communicate with these subpersonalities and get them all on the same page with respect to your mission in life.

Before you can explore, transform, and integrate your subpersonalities, it is important for you to first create a safe place within. This safe place will provide unlimited comfort and guidance to assist you in healing the deep wounds of early trauma.

When asked to write her EMI Abundance Song, Gloria told me that she felt stuck. "I have all these gifts," she said, "but I'm still alone." Gloria was a beautiful, talented, successful graphic artist who had a pattern of attracting unavailable men who inevitably abandoned her. She would then become enraged and plummet into despair. It was obvious that Gloria was re-enacting some kind of early trauma. I asked her to describe her first memory of loss:

> When I was around three years old, I had a favorite stuffed animal, Tony the Tiger, that I carried around everywhere I went. He was so worn and dirty and smelly and I loved him more than anything. One day, my mother was cleaning the house in her usual frenzy. I was playing in the kitchen with Tony. Mother was in a foul mood and told me that Tony was disgusting. She grabbed him out of my hands and tossed him into the incinerator. I just remember screaming and shouting until

> I passed out. When I came to, Tony was gone forever. I was devastated for days and felt like I just couldn't go on living. Mother didn't understand. She said it was just a smelly old toy and wanted to buy me a new one. I've never been able to trust anybody since then.

In that moment of trauma, Gloria lost her natural ability to trust and her belief that she was worthy of love and understanding. Gloria grew up in a violent, abusive home. In order to protect herself, she learned to be guarded and suspicious. She developed a false self, whose function was to please others so that she wouldn't be abused or abandoned. From her teenage years on, she developed what she called a "love addiction." She could not tolerate being alone, so she clung to the men in her life until she drove them away.

Gloria used men as a drug to escape from the overwhelming unresolved feelings that continued to emerge through the course of her adult life. She had never acquired effective tools to deal with these feelings. Instead of exploring her feelings and trying to make sense of them, Gloria simply turned to her drug of choice (love obsession). Even after years of therapy, Gloria still did not feel safe being alone. I suggested that she create a safe place within herself where she could sit with the feelings, images, and memories that emerged and witness them rather than be overwhelmed by them; a place where she could eventually call upon her EMI for help.

The following exercise, Create Your Safe-Place Song, is a powerful technique for anyone who has experienced trauma and abandonment early in life.

Create Your Safe-Place Song

Put yourself into a deeply relaxed state using the Musical Relaxation Response exercise. Let yourself travel back in time and allow to emerge any memories, sensations, and images of places where you have felt the most safe. With each new memory, let the colors, sounds, smells, textures, and feelings permeate your entire being. (If you don't have an actual memory of a safe place, you can create one. It can be an image from a childhood storybook, a daydream, or even a favorite poem or movie. Perhaps you are in a castle surrounded by a moat patrolled by a fire-breathing dragon who protects you from all intruders. Or maybe you are in a monastery high in the Himalayas surrounded by wise and loving teachers.) Feel as if you are really there. Let every cell in your body feel the security and safety of this place.

If more than one safe place emerges, take a few minutes to decide which one affords you the most safety, the one you can imagine going back to over and over again. Take additional time to soak in the good energy of this place. When you are ready, slowly come back to ordinary reality. Record in your Music and Sound Awareness Journal all the memories, images, feelings, and insights that came up for you. Be creative—use poetry, drawing, sculpture, or other media to make the essence of your safe place as real as possible.

After you process your experience using a variety of artistic forms, take a few moments to create your Safe-Place Song. Gather your improvisation instruments and explore musically the pulse and rhythms of your safe place, its melody and tonality, sense of harmony, sound and texture, and its structure. Note if there are particular words, phrases, or rhymes that would be appropriate. You may want to record your exploration on tape so that later, you can hear the whole gestalt. If you do not read or write music, you could sketch a visual score like this one created by my student Mary, who asked four friends to improvise background music for her Safe-Place Song using these instruments (you'll notice that together they represent the four elements):

Ocean drum—with a slow breath pulse, like ocean waves

Bodhran (large Irish hand drum)—with a strong, grounded, steady rhythm, like a mountain's heartbeat

Crystal bell bowl—with a slow shimmering pulse, like celestial winds

Temple bells—with fiery joy to highlight the melody

You are always welcome in my heart.

No matter what you do,

There'll always be a place for you.

You are always welcome in my heart.

No matter what you say, I'll always feel this way.

Mary sang the words over the improvised music, conducting her "orchestra" to emphasize significant lyrics. She also recorded an instrumental-only version to use for solace in times of need.

When you are ready, you can either play the entire piece by yourself or enlist the help of musical friends, as Mary did. Make sure that you record every take. You never know which one will be the best rendition.

(Note for nonmusicians: There are easy-to-use keyboards and other electronic instruments with preprogrammed beats, chord progressions, and baselines that you can use in creating EMI songs and improvisations. See Appendix II for more information.)

Once you have created your Safe-Place Song, you can transform an acting-out moment (in which you automatically deal with a conflict or overwhelming feeling by escaping into maladaptive behavior) into a healing moment (in which you become the witness to these overwhelming thoughts and feelings) and reconnect with your core self.

Musical Time-Out

Take time to notice when you feel overwhelmed by difficult feelings and inner chaos. Behavioral cues include a sense of hopelessness or panic, the desire to escape through your drug of choice, the desire to hurt yourself or others, emotional numbness, confusion, and depersonalization (feeling not real, disconnected from your core self). Take a time-out and find a place where you can be quiet for a few moments. Listen to your Safe-Place Song and recreate the experience of being totally safe and secure. If, after listening to your song, you still feel overwhelmed, practice Breath Awareness until your breathing becomes more still and rhythmic.

Once you feel grounded and relaxed, become the witness to your thoughts, feelings, and memories. Try not to identify with anything that comes up—just watch. Welcome any insights or guidance for your Higher Self that can help in resolving your problem. The feelings, thoughts, and images will pass if you allow yourself to remain the witness.

Music as a Transitional Object

As mentioned earlier, at a significant point in your emotional development, it was necessary for you to have a transitional object, such as a blanket or stuffed animal, that was completely yours and that allowed you to develop a self separate from Mom and Dad.[3] Many people (like Gloria) who were traumatized as children were never permitted transitional objects. Without the opportunity to explore your emotional world through creative play in a safe environment, you may have ended up feeling unreal, perhaps not quite knowing who you were. If this was your experience, it might be difficult for you to access EMI at this point in your life.

Choosing an Instrument as Your Transitional Object

If any of this sounds familiar to you, please know that it is never too late to develop a relationship with the innately creative part of you and discover your true self.

For example, it is not uncommon for adults of all ages to choose a musical instrument as a kind of transitional object. Taking up an instrument is a wonderful way to ignite your creativity and expand your expressive capacity. Consider forming a playful relationship with a relatively easy-to-play instrument: a recorder, hand drum, harmonica, tin whistle, piano, or any other instrument that attracts you.

Here are a few points to keep in mind: Your instrument should be played only by you. You are not required to take lessons. (If you do, choose a teacher who is comfortable with improvisation and humane in his or her approach.) Your instrument is only for personal self-expression; therefore it should be able to hold the depth of your feelings, no matter what you are going through, and capable of expressing a range of emotions without being destroyed. It should allow you to safely explore different moods, desires, feelings without the fear of rejection or annihilation. (Note: Using your primary instrument as a transitional object may be contraindicated if you are a professional musician who started playing music at a very young age. You may want to select a completely different instrument or choose another medium that is relatively conflict free, such as dance, sculpture, or the martial arts.)

The secret to bonding with your transitional object is time. It is important to make some time each day to get to know your instrument, both through technical study and improvisation, and to find new ways of expressing yourself. You might be impatient at first, particularly if the instrument is awkward to play. With gentle guidance and diligent practice, however, you will start hearing things that you would never have believed you could express.

Taking time to be with your instrument is an invitation to your inner child to come out and play. Children need unstructured play time. They also love figuring things out by themselves (like how a harmonica works or how a frame drum is made). If you were stifled as a child and forced to grow up before your time, your inner child will be so grateful. During your play periods, it is important to really listen to the child within. He has been waiting so long to be heard—to be free.

As you continue to explore your relationship with your musical transitional object, you will inevitably open deep channels of emotion that the child in you was never allowed to feel. When this happens, *do not stop playing!* This is a very good time to seek out the help of a professional therapist or counselor who can be with you as you go through this cleansing period. As you continue to play, you will undoubtedly become aware of your Essential Musical Intelligence, which you can then call upon as a self-reflecting transformational tool.

Voice as Transitional Object

Your voice can also be your transitional object.[4] Singing is the most direct way to contact your inner child. Many traumatized individuals, however, are afraid to sing, especially if they were repeatedly forced as children to swallow painful emotions and words. Singing naturally opens the heart and throat chakras, the centers most associated with EMI. Unfortunately, these energy centers are often closed in people who have unresolved issues around early trauma. (A word of caution: when exploring the inner dimensions through musical improvisation—both vocal and instrumental—traumatic symptoms and memories can be activated. If you feel overwhelmed or consistently blocked, please seek professional help.)

If you would like to try using your voice as your transitional object, be gentle at first. Start by practicing toning exercises daily for several weeks to get to know your sound and your vocal capacity. When you are ready to go deeper, you can practice the Child Song exercise to create a secure musical space for your inner child to sing her story.

Child Song

Find a time and space where you know you will not be disturbed. Start by laying down a simple harmonic or rhythmic vamp (see page 155) on a harmonic or percussion instrument. It can be either prerecorded or live. Once you feel the pulse of the vamp, allow yourself to vocally improvise by singing or making sounds what you feel in the moment. Don't be afraid to take risks. Explore the range of your voice and emotions. You are safe in the music. You may feel silly at first, but eventually you will make contact with your inner child. Record each session and listen back. You will be surprised and moved by what you hear.

One of my clients, a jazz bassist, practiced this technique for several weeks. Marty told me that he felt like he was channeling the real-life story of his wounded inner child. The singing brought up intense, long-buried feelings of grief, rage, and longing associated with the death of his mother when he was seven years old. After many years of being blocked creatively, Marty finally unlocked the doors to his heart and throat chakras. He began to feel alive again. He recorded these sessions and ultimately used much of the improvised material to create a song cycle that he titled, "Songs for My Children."

If improvisation seems too threatening for you, singing popular songs that relate to your own personal story are just as good.[5]

One of my clients became fixated on the song, "I Love You, Porgy" from the Gershwin opera, *Porgy and Bess.* (The song is about a troubled woman who desperately needs rescue from a violent, abusive lover.) I asked Carla to bring the song to her next session so that we could explore her feelings about it. The following week, Carla brought the CD and told me that she was ready to "face the music." After only a few moments of listening, Carla burst into tears and sobbed uncontrollably throughout the whole song; she had no words to describe her feelings. I suggested that Carla memorize the lyrics and sing them to my accompaniment during her next session.

The following week, Carla reported that she had sung the

song along with the record every day and had never cried so much in her life. But, she added, she was also feeling much lighter than she had ever felt before. When she sang the song during her session, the trigger phrases were "Don't let him handle me and drive me mad," and "If you can keep me, I want to stay here with you forever, and I'll be so glad." In our subsequent sessions, I learned that Carla, a recovering alcoholic, had been abandoned by her father early in life and was later sexually abused by her mother's live-in boyfriend. Because it was not safe for her to express the terror, grief, anger, and rage related to these frightening occurrences, they were locked up inside her for almost thirty years. Carla was finally ready to tell her story and face the once unbearable pain of abandonment, betrayal, and sexual violation and move on with her life. Subsequently, Carla brought in several other songs that allowed her wounded inner child to speak her truth. Through her courageous song work, she began to connect with her Essential Musical Intelligence, which helped fill with the light of her true self the painful emptiness associated with her wounds.

Classical music can also serve as a transitional object. Sufi master Pir Vilayat Khan tells the story of the death of his beloved fiancée in a motorcycle accident when they were both quite young. He was unable to eat or sleep for weeks; nothing could console his grief. One day, in the depths of despair, he put on a recording of Bach's B Minor Mass. He sobbed throughout the entire piece. For several months, he made a practice of listening to the mass religiously. Gradually he regained his spirit and was able to move on with his life. Pir stated that had it not been for the B Minor Mass, he doesn't know what would have become of him.[6] Although he could never replace his beloved fiancée, Pir realized that he could rely on Bach's music with its archetypal message of hope and transcendence as his steady companion for as long as he needed it.

Tears, the Royal Road to EMI

The expression of grief is, paradoxically, the royal road to awakening EMI. Your tears are an expression of pure love, of the divine child within who naturally expects to be loved, cared for, and nurtured by beneficent others. If you did not feel love for yourself, for others, or for the Divine, you would not cry. For some people, it is very difficult to grieve. They judge their tears as self-indulgent, childish, dramatic, a sign of weakness. Men in particular are told not to cry because it isn't manly. How many of us have closed our hearts because we haven't allowed ourselves to grieve, because it wasn't safe to be so vulnerable? Crying is cleansing. Tears actually contain natural painkillers, along with the remains of stress hormones that can become toxic if not released. That is why we often feel so much better after a good cry.

Crying not only opens the heart chakra, but the throat chakra—the center of expression—as well. When we repress feelings, the throat chakra is closed. In this state we are unable to tap into EMI, the force within us that carries the wisdom and guidance of our higher selves. We are unable to receive our divine inheritance. Weeping makes room for the soul to enter, and it creates space for true expression. Although you may feel that there are no words to express the depths of your sadness, sometimes it does help to talk, or better yet, to sing about it. Once you begin to release the specific traumatic memories from your belly, heart, and throat, new energy flows into your life and change is indeed possible.

Once you have connected with your safe place, composed your Safe-Place Song, and bonded with your musical transitional object, you are on the road to deep emotional healing. There is more work to be done, however. Even though your core self desires healing and integration, if you experienced early trauma, abuse, or abandonment, there are probably subpersonalities who are terrified of growth and change and who work tirelessly to maintain the status quo. These subpersonalities (or "subs," as one of my students calls them), are associated with our early needs for safety and survival. Because the subs are usually fixated at primitive levels of emotional intelligence, they often sabotage our sincere adult efforts toward success, intimacy, radiant health, and self-realization.

As I mentioned earlier, the subs (the abused little girl, introjected parental imagos, and the inimitable false self who strives for absolute perfection) are often frozen at the time of the original trauma. In addition, within every abused person there exists a "victim" sub (the part that feels defeated and powerless) and a "perpetrator" sub (the part that acts out defensively through violence). At certain points over the course of development, the victim sub inevitably identifies with the perpetrator in order to survive. In psychological language this is called "identification with the aggressor." Often this dynamic is unconscious in the traumatized individual and gets acted out either in somatization (the body attacking itself) and/or through passive-aggressive acts.

How do we become aware of our subpersonalities and allow them to safely express what they need so that they can be integrated back into the core self? Witnessing is a powerful tool for uncovering the parts of ourselves that sabotage our growth. Behaviors expressed in a mood of fear, shame, hatred, violence, greed, or envy often reflect negative subpersonalities. These powerful emotions can be difficult to halt once you are caught in their grip, but with determination and discipline, you can stop and become the witness before real damage is done.

Since subpersonalities influence our lives on both the interpersonal and intrapersonal levels, be careful to watch for them in all relational activities as well as in your own personal desires and activities.

For example, if as a child you were deprived of love and emotional bonding with your parents, you might develop a deprived-child sub who always feels empty and has to constantly fill herself with food, shopping, or intense drama (novels, movies, chaotic relationships) to feel safe. Perhaps your parents were very poor and showed disdain for wealthy folks. As a result, you might fear abundance and push away individuals and opportunities that would enhance your success. Maybe you were quite talented as a dancer early in life. Your parents or teachers may have pushed you into dancing professionally before you were ready, giving you no choice but to develop a false-self sub in order to cope with the stress. This sub constantly pushes you toward perfection, even though you know that it is okay for you to take it easy sometimes and just be yourself. These incongruities between your core self (the part that knows who you are and feels unconditionally loved and supported) and your subs (the parts that are fear-based and limited) can create an emotional roller coaster that drains your energies and leads to depression and despair.

Make an effort now to take the witness stance and become aware of when you are operating out of a constricted, negative, or destructive mindset. Take note of what is going on and how you get triggered, and use your Music and Sound Awareness Journal to record these episodes. You will find that the ancillary thoughts, feelings, desires, and attitudes can be attributed to one or more of your wayward subs. See if you can pinpoint and name specific debilitating subpersonalities that get in the way of your personal joy and mastery.

After practicing the witnessing exercise for several weeks as a way of exploring the emptiness associated with her love addiction, Gloria discovered the following subs that were holding her back from achieving joy, intimacy, and success in her life:

1. *Demon Child*–the destructive five-year-old who wreaks havoc in order to get attention. She tries to destroy all of the important adult things that I create because she feels that she will lose me if I am successful. She needs my attention 24/7; she never feels like she has enough.

2. *Raging Teen*–favorite expression, "Just leave me alone!" This sub says hurtful things; controls others with rage; hates her mother and everyone else; fears intimacy, sex and love; is angry all the time.

3. *Fragile One*–the needy three-year-old who is always fearful, desperate for love, ashamed, cries deeply, assumes fetal position when she feels rejected, will say anything in order to be loved, is relieved when conflicts are resolved, and wants to be married, protected, and safe.

Gloria also took time to become aware of some of her core-self attributes—the powerful forward-moving aspects of herself that both she and her friends admire:

1. *Goddess*–powerful partner in love relationships.

2. *Beloved Friend*–loyal, wise friend and mentor who delights in her friends' happiness.

3. *Free Spirit*–very creative; unfettered and unbound.

4. *Hyper-focused Professional*–devoted to clients, selfless servant and creative artist.

Once Gloria delineated and named her subpersonalities, she could begin to know them better, allow them to come out of hiding, and find ways of meeting their needs and gaining their trust. She could also develop her positive core attributes in order to guide and nurture the less-fortunate subs.

One way of getting to know subpersonalities is to give them opportunities to express themselves through spontaneous singing. I asked Gloria to let each sub tell its story through vocal improvisation using the Child Song technique. She began with the most destructive, her Demon Child. Gloria created a background vamp on her keyboard. Then, after tuning into the essence of the sub and literally *becoming* her, she began to sing effortlessly, as if this child had waited a lifetime to be heard. In a voice devoid of emotion—rather cold and empty, with a machinelike rhythm—she sang her desire to destroy all things good the way she had been destroyed. This was the incredibly disturbing voice of the child whose spirit had been mutilated by years of abuse and neglect.

A few weeks later, Gloria was ready to explore the Raging Teen. Similarly, this sub was more than ready to unfold her story. In a voice that was loud, extremely angry, and out of control, the Raging Teen screamed to be listened to. She sang about her need for someone strong enough to help her cope with her crazy feelings instead of punishing her or telling her to shut up.

Following work with her other subs, Gloria was amazed by the distinctive musical characteristics that colored each and surprised by the intensity of the emotions that emerged from the music. Gloria recorded all her improvisations. I asked her to listen back and pull out a key phrase that expressed the essence of each sub. She later used these in activating the Giving-and-Receiving Feedback Loop.

Gloria's Key Song Phrases

Demon Child–"I'm your demon child; I'm running wild. Anything you love, I will destroy. I am Mommy. I've got to be good to Mom. I don't care if it breaks anything you want."

Raging Teen–"I need people who value going through conflicts and can stand it, and when I screw up, I don't have to kill myself."

Fragile One–"Please don't desert me in my hour of need. Show me how to be needed."

The improvisations of Gloria's subpersonalities are filled with gut-wrenching emotions, the kinds that are often submerged and experienced only in altered states. Yet these emotions need to be externalized before true change can occur. The Child Song technique is a powerful way to give these subs a safe place to be.

While finishing up her song cycle, Gloria had a spontaneous Musical Tantra experience (resolution of polarities through musical improvisation) and came up with another song, which she called "Humbled Again." Its key phrase (from her core self) was, "Amen, Amen, I'm humbled again. Please show me the way to surrender and pray." While singing this song, a wave of love and compassion filled Gloria from the depths of her being. She was awed and grateful and knew that she could eventually use this nascent energy to transform her needy subpersonalities.

Once you are familiar with the music of your subpersonalities, you can activate the Giving-and-Receiving Feedback Loop to better understand your subs and give them exactly what they need. This exercise can facilitate deep healing and transformation of your developmentally arrested subpersonalities.

It is different from the Musical Tantra exercise, which employs EMI to resolve universal archetypal polarities. The feedback-loop technique focuses primarily on the exploration and resolution of developmental arrests that result from early trauma. These arrests, as manifested in the inharmonious behavior of wayward subpersonalities, can cripple interpersonal relationships and self-concept.

Giving and Receiving Feedback Loop with Subs

PART I - Identify and give voice to each subpersonality.

Create a musical motif that identifies each *negative* sub.
Create a musical motif that identifies each *positive* sub.
Learn to discriminate between different subs when they dominate your personality.
What are the strengths and weaknesses of each?
Memorize each sub's musical motif.
Which negative sub can be helped by which positive sub?
Make a drawing or collage that represents the essence of each subpersonality (both positive and negative). You could also find an object (doll, stuffed animal, etc.) that strongly reminds you of a particular sub.

PART II - Activate the Giving-and-Receiving Feedback Loop for each sub.

Start with the most needy sub. Place the sub drawing or object on a chair in front of you and gather your improvisation instruments. Activate the impersonal stance and tune into the energy of the needy sub. Choose an instrument (or use your voice) to give this subpersonality what it needs. Let yourself receive communication back from the sub. You will know that you have completed the loop when you experience a shift in energy. You should feel deeply calm, centered, and awed by the power of this process. (Note: While playing, you might receive more information about your sub, i.e. its reason for being, memories, or insights about what it may need from you. Be sure to record these insights in your journal to help you in future work.)

You might need to work with a particular sub more than once. You'll know your work has been successful when you see a change in the attitude and feeling tone of the sub. You will also experience a qualitative change in your relationship with yourself and others.

Allow some time to pass—anywhere from one to four weeks—before you work with another subpersonality. The amount of time depends on the rate of change you experience with the first sub.

You can also use the role-playing technique, in which you enlist the aid of a close friend or therapist to play the needy-sub role. Do this if you are particularly frightened of one or more of your subs. Make this experience as safe and comfortable as you possibly can.

Because the Giving-and-Receiving Feedback Loop requires a shift into an altered state of consciousness, it is important to *ground and center yourself afterward.* If your interaction with a subpersonality was particularly difficult or left you feeling vulnerable, surround yourself with white light before moving on to other activities. This will allow you to feel protected and safe.

Gloria chose the Giving-and-Receiving Feedback Loop to work with her Raging Teen. As she drew a portrait of herself at about age fourteen, she recalled occasions when she was given confusing mixed messages by her mother. For example, her mother wanted her to look beautiful, but then one day, without discussion, chopped off Gloria's prized long hair. Gloria's mother also wanted her to be thin, yet forced her to eat large portions of meat and carbohydrates. Additionally, Gloria was told that sex was forbidden at her age, yet she had to listen to her mother talk obsessively about the details of her romance novels. In adding the final touch to her portrait, Gloria drew a large *A* (for achievement) across her chest signifying that even though she did everything right and got the highest grades in school, it still wasn't enough to please her parents.

Feeling helpless and hopeless after confronting these memories, Gloria placed her self-portrait on a chair in front of her. In order to ground and center herself, she practiced breath awareness followed by several rounds of alternate-nostril breathing. As her mind-body became more still, Gloria entered the impersonal stance. She took a couple of minutes to tune into the Raging Teen self-portrait. She then selected a large crystal gong and began to play.

As she dragged the beater around the edge of the bowl, producing a lovely rich singing tone, more images surfaced. She relived the memory of her mother's frequent double message, "I love you and now I'm gonna hit you." However, Gloria now felt safe, held by the strong resonating music. She later explained, "The music allowed me to see what was so distorted in my teen years, and at the same time, what would have been right." The music functioned as both witness and loving container for Gloria's wounded subpersonality.

After the feedback-loop exercise, Gloria realized that the Raging Teen needed a safe place where she wouldn't be judged or rejected in order to share her overwhelming feelings. She also discovered that her sub needed someone who could model gentle yet firm self-discipline rather than threats and manipulation. Gloria suddenly remembered her favorite piano teacher, who had moved away when she was eight. "Mrs. Spader really enjoyed my music and encouraged me to learn with love, not fear." I suggested that Gloria emulate Mrs. Spader's mentoring style whenever her Raging Teen needed guidance or discipline.

The following steps will help you in subsequent sessions to refine your ability to use the feedback loop to contact, heal, and integrate your subpersonalities back into the whole of your being.

1. See if you can determine the developmental age of your sub. This will help you to understand why she acts the way she does. For example, if your sub is between the ages of two and seven years old, her perception of reality is egocentric and her thoughts concrete—things are either black or white, all good or all bad. She probably also has limited role-taking and communication abilities. Once you realize how emotionally undeveloped this sub is, you can be more accepting and compassionate and take the responsibility as an adult centered in your core self to patiently reparent her. A couple of good books that will help you understand the key developmental issues of life are *Homecoming: Reclaiming and Championing Your Inner Child,* and *Bradshaw on: The Family,* both by recovery expert John Bradshaw.[7]

2. Clearly determine what the sub needs from you to help her grow, and offer it whenever she attempts to take control.

3. Help your sub develop a relationship with a higher power. Many traumatized children become cynical and angry at God. You can help your young subs deal with these feelings by introducing more beauty into your life: allow ample time to revel in the majesty, peace, harmony, and perfection of nature, the purest aspect of Absolute Being. Take regular time-outs to relax in the music and imagery of your safe place. The more safety you can create in your inner world, the more your subs will be free to trust in their Higher Power.

4. Give your sub an opportunity to safely explore feelings of hate, rage, and grief. All children need a safe place to vent painful feelings. Use the Child Song and feedback-loop techniques. As painful feelings are acknowledged and released, poison (pain and limitation) is turned into medicine.

Mantra Meditation and EMI

When all is said and done, there is still one EMI practice that is deceptively simple but wonderfully effective in transforming the wounds of abuse and abandonment. It can be used alone or with the other exercises in this book. That practice is mantra meditation. It involves repeating a *mantra* (universal divine seed-syllable) internally over and over with complete concentration until your mind merges with the essence of the mantra and achieves a state of deep peace and equilibrium. The power of mantra meditation comes from the divine essence inherent within the mantra itself. By repeating this word throughout your meditation session and throughout the day, you reprogram your unconscious mind to radiate the essence of the mantra instead of the flux of thoughts and feelings that keep you mired in the ego.[8] When dealing with the fears, numbness, hostility, and despair associated with past trauma, repeating your mantra can instantly bring you back to your true self. Its effects are cumulative. The more you repeat your mantra, especially during times when you feel possessed by negative subpersonalities, the more you achieve spiritual power to transform your life and reach higher states of consciousness.

Although many people receive personal mantras during formal initiation ceremonies, you can also achieve deep meditation with a powerful universal mantra, *so-ham*. According to Hindu mystics, so-ham, meaning "I am that," is the natural sound of your breath. ("So" is inhalation, and "ham" is the exhalation.) Renowned Hindu yogi Sri Swami Rama explains, "You breathe that great cosmic energy, the energy that gives us birth, and through that breath you are linked to the Divine."[9] According to Rama, there is only one energy source in which we all have our roots, and so-ham gradually awakens us to it. As we realize this essential truth, Rama argues, there is no need for judgment, greed, fear, and suffering.

Mantra Meditation

Practice mantra meditation at the same time and place each day. Some people like to meditate first thing in the morning; others prefer bedtime. Be consistent so that daily meditation makes a permanent groove in your mind. Choose a comfortable place where you will not be disturbed.

First practice a brief relaxation exercise, then a few rounds of alternate-nostril breathing, followed by a few minutes of Breath Awareness. When you feel relaxed, grounded, and focused, silently breathe in SO as you inhale, and breath out HAM on your exhalation. Continue for about twenty minutes. If thoughts, feelings, or other distractions emerge, just let them pass and bring your focus back to the mantra. In time, your thoughts quiet down, your breathing becomes slower and deeper, and you gradually feel more calm and serene.

Mantra meditation cuts through all the sheaths, leading to the peace at the core of your being. You can achieve peace throughout the day by silently repeating the mantra during all of your activities. With practice, you will become one with your essential nature, which is peace, bliss, and happiness. Meditation helps you to realize that identifying with the objects of the mind has nothing to do with your essential nature. The more your mind moves toward silence, the more creative and dynamic it becomes. Mantra meditation also soothes the nervous system and increases vitality, and is a perfect complement to all the EMI techniques. As your mantra meditation practice deepens, you will naturally begin to loosen your ego attachments and realize that you are simply a wave in the ocean of bliss. You are free from all fears, knowing that the center of consciousness—the source of your Essential Musical Intelligence—is within you.

When you have penetrated each of the sheaths with the illuminating sword of your Essential Musical Intelligence, you become one with the self—your true essence. In this state of being, you attain perfect wisdom. There is no more for you to learn, nothing more for you to do. Surely you have had flashes of this transcendent consciousness while exploring the exercises in this book. With continued practice, you will experience more extended periods of pure consciousness until the realization of self becomes your only reality.

Hazrat Inayat Khan, the great Persian classical musician and Sufi master, reached this state of being through his deeply spiritual relationship with music:

> I first believed without hesitation in the existence of the soul, and then I wondered about the secret of its nature. I persevered and strove in search of my soul, and found at last that I myself was the cover over my soul. I realized that that in me which believed and that in me which wondered, that which persevered in me, and that which found, and that which was found at last, was no other than my soul. I thanked the darkness that brought me to the light, and I valued the veil which prepared for me the vision in which I saw myself reflected, the vision produced in the mirror of my soul. Since then I have seen all souls as my soul, and realized my soul as the soul of all; and what bewilderment it was when I realized that I alone was, if there were anyone; that I am whatever and whoever exists; and that I shall

> be whoever there will be in the future. And there was no end to my happiness and joy. Verily, I am the seed and I am the root and I am the fruit of this tree of life.[10]

Khan's words suggest that it is indeed possible to achieve a state of pure consciousness and bliss through lifelong devotion to music. Allow music to be your friend and guide throughout life's journey. Let your Essential Musical Intelligence lead you home.

Appendix I:

Exercise Finder

Appendix I

Appendix II:

Resources

Musical Equipment

For nonmusicians: to create background music for your Lullaby, Abundance Song, Soul Song, Safe-Place Song, the following equipment is ideal (and inexpensive):

Qchord: Digital Songcard Guitar by Suzuki
Yamaha DD35 Digital Drums
Roland MC303 Drum machine/analog synth

Keyboards

Casio Keyboards: many to choose from; most have a variety of interesting rhythmic beats and grooves; easy-to-play chord progressions

Yamaha also makes a good portable keyboard:
Yamaha DJX2 contemporary beats; easy to play

Music-Making Software Programs for Nonmusicians

For Mac users: Metasynth by UI Software; integrated sequencing synthesis and sound design for those who are visually inclined; you can actually paint in sound

For PC users: Reason, by Propeller Heads; all-in-one sampler, midi sequencer and virtual analog synth

Acoustic/Ethnic Instruments

For congas: Latin Percussion, Inc., www.lpmusic.com

For "ocean" and hand drums: Remo, Inc., www.remo.com

For Expert Advice on Choosing Musical Instruments for Therapeutic Purposes

Joe Piccinnini, MA, MT-BC, Director
Richmond Music Center
25 Page Avenue • Staten Island, NY 10309
Phone: 718-967-4686
www.richmondmusiccenter.com

Kirsten Nelson, MA, MT-BC,
Music therapy consultant
West Music
P. O. Box 5521, 1212 Fifth Street • Coralville, IA 52241-0521
800-397-9378
www.westmusic.com

Music Therapy

American Music Therapy Association
8455 Colesville Road
Suite 930 • Silver Spring, MD 20910
301-589-3300
Music Therapy information and resources

Music-Related Associations

Music Educators National Conference (MENC)
Info on all aspects of music education
www.menc.org

National Association of Music Merchants

Promotes music education; research on music and the brain
www.namm.com

Musicians' Wellness, Inc.
Nonprofit music therapy organization dedicated to meeting the mental and behavioral health needs of professional musicians
www.musicianswellness.org

Training in Yoga, Meditation, and Self-Transformation

Himalayan International Institute of
Yoga Science and Philosophy of the USA
RR I Box 400 • Honesdale, PA 18431
www.HimalayanInstitute.org

Music and Imagery

Association for Music and Imagery
P. O. Box 4286 • Blaine, WA 98231-4486
360-756-8096
Jim Rankin, Executive Secretary
Information on GIM; professional training programs nationwide

Books on Music Therapy and Music Healing

MMB Music, Inc.
Contemporary Arts Building
3526 Washington Avenue • St. Louis, MO 63103
314-531-9635
www.mmbmusic.com

Improvisation Workshops

Music for People
376 Newtown Turnpike • Redding, CT 06896
203-938-0367
Improvisation workshops led by cellist David Darling

Healthy Sounds
Barry Bernstein, Director
P. O. Box 40304 • Overland Park, KS 66204
913-888-5517
Percussion-based music improvisation workshops
www.healthysounds.com

For more information on training seminars, workshops, classes, and consultations with Dr. Louise Montello, please log on to: **www.essentialmusicalintelligence.com** or call/write:

4 Washington Square Village
Suite 13J • New York, NY 10012
Phone/fax: 212-473-8753

The following EMI CDs and tapes by Louise Montello are also available for sale at the above site:

Music of the Five Elements
Music for Balancing Breath/Energy Currents
EMI Breathing/Relaxation Exercises (with improvised EMI music in background)
Toning the Five Elements

Guided EMI Meditation Series:

Opening Your Heart
Creating Abundance
Opening to Creativity
Overcoming Anxiety
Antidote to Procrastination
Overcoming Addictions
Your Safe Place Meditation
Ambient EMI Music for the Workplace
EMI Music for Dogs
EMI Music for Cats

Appendix III: *Suggestions for Music Imagery Tapes*

The Music of Love

Felix Mendelssohn, *Symphony No. 4, Italian* (Maag–MCA; Davis–Philips)
Gustav Mahler, "Adagietto," from *Symphony No. 2* (Previn–Angel)
Gustav Mahler, "Adagietto," from *Symphony No. 5* (Kubelik–DGG)
Andre Messager, *The Two Pigeons* (Lanchbery–EMI)
Richard Wagner, "Liebestod," from *Tristan und Isolde,* Romantic Adagio (Karajan–DGG)
J. S. Bach, "Air on the G String," from *Bach's Greatest Hits* (BMG Classics)

The Music of Courage

Vangelis, *Chariots of Fire,* soundtrack (Polydor)
Charles Gounod, "Sanctus," from *Saint Cecilia Mass* (Norman, Gibson–Philips)
Unfold Ye Portals of Creation (Mormon Tabernacle Choir, Ormandy–Columbia)
Marisa Robles, *The Narnia Suite* (EMI)
Ludwig van Beethoven, *Leonore Overture No. 3; Egmont Overture* (Karajan–DGG)
Joonas Kokkonen, *Requiem* (Soderblom–Finlandia)

The Music of Light

Alexander Gretchaninov, *Holy Radiant Light* (Ottley–Columbia)
The Sufi Choir Sings Kabir (Cold Mountain Music)

Giuseppe Verdi, "Sanctus," from *Requiem* (Reiner–London)
Eugene Friesen, Paul Halley, *Cathedral Pines* (Living Music)
Herbert Howells, *Hymns of Paradise* (Willcocks–EMI)

The Music of Creativity

Daniel Kobialka, "Sleepers Awake" and "Sheep May Safely Graze"(J. S. Bach) from *Daniel Kobialka Performs* (Li–Sem)
Georges Bizet, *Symphony in C* (Beecham–EMI)
Cesar Franck, *Psyche* (Strauss–Connoisseur Society)
Henry Mancini, "Meggie's Theme" and "The Thorn Birds Theme," from *In the Pink* (Galway, Mancini–RCA)

Music for Peace

J. S. Bach, "Largo," from *Concerto for Two Violins in D Minor* (Lautenbacher, Vorholz–Allegro); and *Jesu Joy of Man's Desiring* (Baroque Masterpieces–Sony)
Georgia Kelly, *Sound of Spirit* (Heru, Box 954, Topanga, CA 90290)
Jules Massenet, *Meditation on Thais* (Karajan–DGG)
Paul Hindemith, "Concert of Angels," from *Mathis de Maler Symphony* (Ormandy–Columbia)
Ralph Vaughan Williams, *Symphony No. 3, Pastoral* (Previn–RCA)

The Music of Nurturing

Johannes Brahms, *Symphony No. 2*, first movement (Jochum–EMI)
Zdenek Fibich, *Symphony No. 3* (Belohlavek–Supraphon)
Ludwig van Beethoven, *Symphony No. 2*, second movement (Jochum–EMI)
Ralph Vaughn Williams, *Rhosymedre* Prelude
Giacomo Puccinni, *Madama Butterfly*, Humming Chorus

Gabriel Faure, *Sanctus; Pie Jesu,* from *Requiem* (Hendricks, Plasson–EMI)
Guiseppe Torelli, *Concerti Grossi* (Faerber–Turnabout)

The Music of Longing

Victor Herbert, *Ah, Sweet Mystery of Life* (Sills, Kostelanetz–Angel)
Aaron Copland, *Fanfare for the Common Man* (Ormandy–Columbia); *A Lincoln Portrait* (Carl Sandburg, Kostelanetz–Columbia)
Alban Berg, *Violin Concerto* (Suk, Ancerl–Quintessence)
Peter Ilich Tchaikovsky, "Andante," from *Symphony No. 5* (Ormandy–Delos)
Frederic Chopin, *Nocturne, Opus 9, No. 2* (Ormandy–Columbia)

The Music of Discontent

Franz Joseph Haydn, *Sinfonia Concertante* (Ristenpart–Nonesuch)
Sergei Rachmaninov, *Piano Concerto No. 3* (Horowitz, Ormandy–RCA)
Thomas Arne, *Overtures* (Hogwood–Oiseau)
Gaetano Donizetti, *Miserere* (Maklari–Hungaroton)
Gandhi, soundtrack (Jarre–RCA)

The Music of Joy

Gustav Mahler, *Symphony No. 4,* fourth movement (Blegen, Levine–RCA)
Maurice Ravel, "The Fairy Garden," from *Mother Goose* (Martinson–RCA)
Wolfgang Amadeus Mozart, *Coronation Mass* (Ristenpart–Nonesuch)
Cesar Franck, *Redemption* (Barenboim–DGG)
Ernest Bloch, "Rejoicing," from *Baal Shem* (Mordkovitch, Gerhardt–RCA)
Daniel Kolbialka, *Path of Joy* (Li–Sem Enterprises)

The Music of Healing

Frederick Delius, *Florida Suite* (Beecham–EMI)
Wolfgang Amadeus Mozart, *Violin Concerto No. 3,* slow movement (Stern, Szell–Columbia)
Franz Joseph Haydn, Choruses from *The Creation* (Willcocks–EMI)
Sir Arthur Sullivan, *The Lost Chord* (McCormack–RCA)
Yo-Yo Ma, *The Cello Suites Inspired by Bach* (Sony)
Johann Pachelbel, *Canon and Gigue for 3 Violins and Basso Continuo in D* (Baroque Masterpieces–Sony)

The Music of Union

Daniel Kolbialka, *Coral Seas, Vivaldi, Largo* (Li–Sem)
Ralph Vaughan Williams, *Sine Nomine: For All the Saints* (Choir of St. Luke's Church, San Francisco–Wilson Audiophile)
Serge Rachmaninov, *Vespers* (Rostropovich–Erato)
Aaron Copland, *Suite from Our Town; Quiet City* (Abravanel–Vanguard)
Michael Jones, *Wind and Whispers* (Sona Gaia)

Music for Focusing

Ludwig van Beethoven, *Violin Concerto in D* (Mutter, Karajan–DGG)
Franz Joseph Haydn, *Flute Quartets* (Rampal–Seraphim); *The Heilig Mass* (Marriner–Argo)
Patrick Ball, *Secret Isles* (Fortuna); *From a Distant Time* (Fortuna)
Antonio Salieri, *Sinfonia in D* (Marzendorfer–Musical Heritage)
J. S. Bach, *The Goldberg Variations* (Landowska–RCA); *Fugue in A Minor, Fantasies and Fugues* (Masaaki Suzuki–BIS)
Wolfgang Amadeus Mozart, *Sonata for Two Pianos in D Major* (De Larrocha, Previn–RCA)

Music for Cleansing

Antonio Vivaldi, *Flute Concertos* (Rampal, Scimone–Columbia)
Francis Poulenc, *Concert Champetre–Rustic Concerto* (Van de Wiele, Pretre–Angel)
Evenson, *High Joy* (Soundings of the Planet)
Ennio Morricone, *The Mission* (London Philharmonic–Virgin)

Music to Release Blocked Energy

Ludwig van Beethoven, *Symphony No. 7,* fourth movement (Karajan–DGG)
Antonin Dvorak, *Piano Quartet in D* (Suk–Pro Arte)
Claude Bolling, *Guitar Concerto* (Romero, Shearing–Angel)
Ernest Block, *The Voice in the Wilderness* (Starker, Mehta–London)
Ildebrando Pizzetti, *Piano Concerto* (Borini, Alberth–RCA)
Ernest Gold, *Exodus* (Soundtrack–RCA)
Alexander Borodin, "Polovtsian Dances," from *Prince Igor* (Ormandy–Columbia)

Music for Grieving

Alban Berg, Violin Concerto, *To the Memory of an Angel* (Kremer, Davis–Philips)
James Galway, *Song of the Seashore* (Galway, Iwaki–RCA)
Samuel Barber, *Adagio for Strings* (Shippers–Odyssey)
Johannes Brahms, "Quintet for Clarinet and Strings in B Minor," *Complete Quintets* (Berlin Philharmonic–Philips); *German Requiem* (Karajan, Janowitz, Wachter–DGG)
Schindler's List, Soundtrack (John Williams, Itzhak Perlman–MCA)
Maurice Ravel, *Pavane pour une Infante Defunte,* Bolero, (Ozawa, BSO–DGG); Melodies hebraiques (2): no 1, Kaddish (Ravel: Works for Piano, Violin and Cello/Laredo, et al–Arabesque)
J. S. Bach, *Mass in B Minor* (Karajan, Schwarzkopf, et al–EMI)

Music for Contemplation

Marie-Joseph Canteloube, *Songs of the Auvergne* (De Los Angeles, Jacquillat–Angel)
Ludwig van Beethoven, *Symphony No. 9*, third movement (Furtwängler–EMI)
Gustav Mahler, "Adagio," From *Symphony No. 10* (Haitink–Philips)

Music of Imagination

Sergei Prokofiev, *Piano Concerto No. 1* (Graffman–Szell–Columbia)
Henry Mancini, "Meggie's Theme" and "The Thorn Birds Theme," from *In the Pink* (Galway, Mancini–RCA)
Sir Edward Elgar, *Sea Pictures* (Soloist: Dame Janet Baker, Barbirolli–EMI)
Claude Debussy, *Clair de lune; Prelude to the Afternoon of a Faun* (Ormandy–Columbia)
Robert Schumann, *Dreams* (Ormandy–Columbia)
Cesar Franck, *Psyche* (Strauss–Connoisseur Society)
Charles Ives, *Symphony No. 2*, first and third movements (Ormandy–RCA)

Music of Flow

Frederick Delius, *Summer Night on the River* (Beecham–Seraphim)
Franz Joseph Haydn, *Concerto in D* (DeLarrocha, Zinman–London)
Bedrich Smetana, "The Moldau," from *My Country* (Karajan–Angel)

Music for Meditation

Kitaro, *Silk Road Suite* (Canyon Records)
Paul DiVietri, *Partita Teresiana* (Teresiana Records)

Ludwig van Beethoven, *Piano Concertos 1 and 3,* second movements (Perahia, Haintink–Columbia)
J. S. Bach, *Motets* (Willcocks–Argo)

Music of Power

Vangelis, *Chariots of Fire,* soundtrack (Polydor)
Franz Shubert, *Mass No. 6 in E-flat* (St. Johns, Guest–Argo); *Sinfonia Concertante* (Ristenpart–Nonesuch)
Ludwig van Beethoven, *Leonore Overture No. 3; Egmont Overture* (Karajan–DGG)
Sir Arthur Sullivan, *The Lost Chord* (Burrows–London)
Modeste Mussorgsky, "The Great Gate of Kiev," from *Pictures at an Exhibition* (Giulini–DGG)
Richard Strauss, *Alpine Symphony* (Karajan–DGG)
Sir Hubert Parry, *I Was Glad; Jerusalem* (Wicks–Argo)
George Frideric Handel, "Worthy is the Lamb" and final "Amen," from *Messiah* (Ormandy–Columbia)

Music for Problem Solving

Antonin Dvorak, *Piano Quartet in D* (Suk–Pro Arte)
Music of Jubiliee, *J. S. Bach Favorites for Organ and Orchestra* (Biggs, Roznyai–Columbia)
Wolfgang Amadeus Mozart, *Sonata in D Major for Two Pianos*

The Music of Anger

Carl Orff, *Carmina Burana* (Previn–Angel)
Ludwig van Beethoven, *Symphony No. 5 in C Minor* (Klemperer–Angel)
J. S. Bach, *Toccata and Fugue in D,* orchestrated by Leopold Stokowski (Seraphim)
Igor Stravinsky, *Le Sacre du Printemps* (New York Philharmonic, Bernstein–Sony)

Bela Bartok, *String Quartet No. 5*, first movement (Novak Quartet–Philips)

Gustav Holst, "Mars," from *The Planets* (Williams, Strauss/Mehta, Los Angeles–Decca)

Music of Angels

Christopher von Gluck, *Dance of the Blessed Spirits* (Stokowski–Seraphim)

Gabriel Faure, "Sanctus" and "In Paradise," from *Requiem* (Willcocks–Seraphim)

Pablo Casals, *Song of the Birds* (Munroe, Kostelanetz–Columbia)

Paul Horn, *In Concert* (Golden Flute)

Jean Sibelius, *Karelia Overture* (Ormandy–RCA)

Music of Transformation

Gustav Mahler, *Symphony No. 2, Resurrection,* fifth movement (Price, Fassbaldner, Stokowski–RCA)

Anton Bruckner, *Symphony No. 9* (Furtwängler–EMI)

Richard Strauss, *Death and Transfiguration,* for orchestra (Previn–Angel); *Four Last Songs,* for soloist and orchestra (Norman, Masur–Philips)

Hector Berlioz, *Te Deum* (Abbado–DGG)

Music to Stimulate Feelings

A Persian Heritage: Classical Music of Iran (Nonesuch Explorer)

Jan Sibelius, *The Bard* (Berglund–EMI)

Thomas Arne, *Overtures* (Hogwood–Oiseau)

Frederick Delius, *Florida Suite* (Beecham–EMI)

Adolph Wiklund, *Concerto No. 2 for Piano and Orchestra* (Westerberg–Caprice)

Ernest Bloch, *Schelomo, Voice in the Wilderness*/Scalfi (Real Sound)

Jean Cras, *Scenes of Children* (Stoll–Cybelia)

The Music of Nature

Anton Dvorak, *In Nature's Realm* (Kertesz–London)
Paul Horn, *Inside the Powers of Nature* (Golden Flute)
Gustav Mahler, *Symphony No. 4,* third movement (Szell–Columbia)
Jan Sibelius, *Karelia Suite* (Järvi–Bis)
Ludwig van Beethoven, "The Brook," from *Symphony No. 6,* second movement (Jochum–EMI)
Deuter, *Cicada* (Kuckuck–West Germany)

The Music of Sensuality

Richard Wagner, *Tristan und Isolde* (Barenboim, Meier, Jerusalem–Teldec)
Maurice Ravel, *Bolero* (Charles Munch/Boston Symphony–RCA)
Alexander Scriabin, "Poem of Ecstasy," *Great Performers of the Twentieth Century* (Stokowski–BBC Legends)
Karl Goldmark, "In the Garden," from *Rustic Wedding Symphony* (Previn–Angel)

Appendix IV: *Suggestions for Music According to Energy/Breath*

Energy/ Breath	Genre	Artist	Work
PRĀNA	Classical	Ludwig van Beethoven	Moonlight Sonata
	Classical	Ludwig van Beethoven	Piano Concerto No. 5 in E-fla Major Op. 73 Emperor Concert
	Classical	Aaron Copland	Appalachian Spring
	Classical	Giacomo Puccini	Gianni Schicci
	Folk	Simon & Garfunkel	
	Jazz	Miles Davis	
	New Age	Enya	
	Pop	Seal	
APĀNA	Blues	Junior Kimbrough	
	Classical	Antonio Vivaldi	Cello Concerto in E Minor
	Pop	Fleetwood Mac	
	Pop	Cassandra Wilson	
	World		
	World	Ladysmith Black Mambazo	Thula Mtwana
	World	Lucky Dube	My Game
	World	Mickey Hart	
	World	Baba Olatungi	African Drumming
SAMĀNA	Classical	Ludwig van Beethoven	Symphony No. 5 in C Minor Op. 67
	Classical	Anton Bruckner	Symphony No. 8 in C Mino
	Jazz	Freddie Hubbard	

Many of these selections were found in Hal Lingerman's wonderful book, Life Streams: Journeys into Meditaition and Music.

Selection	CD Title	Label
	Beethoven Piano Sonatas	Philips Concert
Adagio	Rubenstein Collection, Vol. 58: Beethoven Piano	RCA Victor Red
	A Copeland Celebration, Vol. I: Orchestral and Chamber Works	Sony Classical
O Mio Bambino Caro	Kiri—Her Greatest Hits—Live	London/Decca
Bridge Over Troubled Water	Greatest Hits	Columbia
Flamenco Sketches	Kind of Blue	Columbia
Caribbean Blue	Shepherds Moons	Reprise
A Kiss from a Rose	2nd Album	Sire
Crawling King Snake	Soul Blues	Fat Possum
Lento Espressivo	Largo—Music for Dreaming	Arte Nova
Gold Dust Woman	Rumours	Warner Bros.
You Don't Know What Love Is	Blue Light 'Til Dawn	Blue Note
Eleggua	Rhythms of Cuban Santeria	Smithsonian Folkways
African Lullaby	Inala	Shanachie
South African Legends	Victims	Shanachie
Island Groove	Planet Drum	RYKODISC
	Drums of Passion	Columbia
Allegro con Brio	Beethoven, et al.: Symphonies	Platinum Entertainment
Finalé	Symphony No. 8 in C Minor	Magic Master
Breaking Point	Breaking Point	Blue Note

Energy/ Breath	Genre	Artist	Work
SAMĀNA	Pop	Marvin Gaye	
	Pop	Pearl Jam	
	Pop	Marilyn Manson	
	Pop	Sting	
UDĀNA	Blues	Otis Redding	
	Classical	Igor Stravinsky	Le Sacre du printemps
	Classical	Antonio Vivaldi	
	Pop	Tori Amos	
	Pop	Whitney and Cissy Houston	
	Pop	Janis Joplin	
	Pop	Brian McKnight	
	Pop	Alanis Morrisette	
	Pop	Stevie Nicks	
	Stage	Jonathon Larson	Rent
VYĀNA	Classical	Ludwig van Beethoven	Symphony No. 6 in F Major Op. 68
	Classical	Claude Debussy	Suite Bergamasque
	Jazz	Miles Davis	
	New Age	Deuter	
	Pop	Tracy Chapman	
	Pop	Marvin Gaye	
	Pop	Pearl Jam	
	Pop	Radiohead	
	Pop	Led Zeppelin	
	Stage	Jonathan Larson	Rent
	World	Sheila Chandra	
	World	Vusi Mahlasela	

Selection	CD Title	Label
Got to Give It Up	The Very Best of Marvin Gaye	UTU
Animal	Vs.	Epic
The Beautiful People	Anti-Christ Superstar	Interscope
A Desert Rose	Brand New Days	China
I Can't Turn You Loose	Live in Europe	Atlantic
Danse Sacrale	Mussorgsky/Karajan	Musikfest
Agitata da due venti	Live in Italy: Thibaudet et al.	London/Decca
Sugar	To Venus and Back	Atlantic
I Knew Him So Well	Whitney	Arista
Down on Me	Janis Joplin in Concert	Columbia
Last Dance	Back at One	Motown
You Oughta Know	Jagged Little Pill	Maverick
Edge of Seventeen	Timespace: Best of Stevie Nicks	Modern
Seasons of Love	Original Broadway Cast	Dream Works
Andante molto mosso	Music for a Stress-Free World	RCA Victor
Clair de lune	Night Songs	London/Decca
All Blues	Kind of Blue	Columbia
Wind & Mountain	Stress Busters—Music for a Stressless World	New Earth
I'm Ready	New Beginning	Elektra
Sexual Healing	Soulful Sound	Sony Classical
Who You Are	No Code	Epic
Paranoid Android	OK Computer	Capitol
Whole Lotta Love	The Song Remains the Same	Swan Song
No Day But Today	Original Broadway Cast	Dream Works
Roots and Wings	Roots and Wings	Narada
Kuyobanjani Na?	South African Legends	Putumayo

Appendix V: *Suggestions for Music According to Element*

Element	Genre	Artist	Work
EARTH	Classical	J. S. Bach	French Suite No. 5 in G M
	Classical	Henryk Górecki	Symphony No. 3 Op. 36 ('7
	Classical	Claudio Monteverdi	Magnificat
	Classical	Igor Stravinsky	The Rite of Spring
	New Age	The Gyuto Monks	
	Pop	Fiona Apple	
	Pop	Lauryn Hill	
	World	Burkina Faso	The Pulse of Life
WATER	Classical	George F. Handel	
	Classical	Lou Harrison	Gamelan Music
	Classical	Thomas Tallis	Spem in Alium
	Folk	James Taylor	
	Jazz	Miles Davis	
	Jazz	Billie Holliday	
	Jazz	Robert Johnson	
	Jazz	Dave Matthews	
	New Age	Paul Horn	
	Pop	Marvin Gaye	
	Rock	Santana	
	World	Phillip Glass	Passages
	World	Friedrich Smetana	My Country
FIRE	Classical	George Bizet	The Pearl Fishers
	Classical	Alexander Borodin	Prince Igor
	Classical	Anton Dvorak	Symphony No. 9 in E Mino Op. 95

Selection	CD Title	Label
Sarabande	Baby Needs Baroque	Delos
Lento	Symphony No. 3	Nonesuch
	A History of Baroque Music—Sacred Music	Harmonia Mundi
Dance of the Earth	Le Sacre du Printemps	Sony Classical
	The Gyuto Monks: Tibetan Tantric Choir	Windham Hill
Slow Like Honey	Tidal	Work Group
The Miseducation of Lauryn Hill	To Zion	Columbia
Sarafina	Global Meditation	Ellipsis Arts
Cara Sposa	Arias	ABC Classics
Gending Alexander	Gamelan Music	Musicmasters
Spem in Alium	Winchester Cathedral Choir	Hyperion
Steam Roller	Best Live	Sony Classical
All Blues	Kind of Blue	Columbia
Can't Help Loving 'Dat Man	This Is Jazz No. 32	Columbia
Kind Hearted Woman	King of Delta Blues	Legacy
Crash into Me	Crash	RCA
Heart IV, VIII	Inside the Taj Mahal	Kuchkuck
Let's Get It On	Great Songs & Performances	Motown
Smooth	Supernatural	Arista
	Original Music Compsd. by Ravi Shankar & Phillip Glass	BMG
Moldau	The Moldau	Angel
Au Fond du Temple Saint	Jussi Björling: "The Pearl Fishers" Duet	RCA Victor
Polovetsian Dances	Splendors of Russian Opera	London/Decca
Allegro confucco	Symphony No. 9 in E Minor Op. 95	London/Decca

Element	Genre	Artist	Work
	Classical	Astor Piazzolla	María de Buenos Aires
	Classical	Gioachino Rossini	La gazza ladra
	Pop	Gloria Estefan	
	Pop	Sergio Mendes	
	Rock	Jimi Hendrix	
	Rock	Pearl Jam	
	Rock	Nine Inch Nails	
	Rock	Rusted Root	
AIR	Classical	J. S. Bach	Brandenburg Concerto No.
	Classical	Ludwig van Beethoven	
	Classical	Ludwig van Beethoven	Romance No. 2 in F Major Op. 50
	Classical	Ludwig van Beethoven	Symphony No. 7 in A Maj Op. 92
	Classical	Gustav Holst	The Planets
	Folk	Joni Mitchell	
	Gospel	Audra McDonald	
	Jazz	John Coltrane	
	Jazz	Sarah Vaughn	
ETHER	Classical	Ian Anderson	Divinities
	Classical	Gustav Holst	The Planets
	Classical	Erik Satie	Gymnopédie
	Classical	Johannes Symonis	Secular Music of the Chantilly Codex
	Jazz	Pat Metheny and Lyle Mays	
	New Age		Gregorian chant
	New Age	Brian Eno	
	New Age	David Garfield	

Selection	CD Title	Label
Yo soy María	María de Buenos Aires	Teldec
Overture	Favorite Opera Overtures	Sony Classical
Get on Your Feet	Cuts Both Ways	CBS
Mas Que Nadar	Foursider	A & M
Stepping Stone	First Rays of the New Rising Sun	MCA
Do the Evolution	Yield	Epic
We're in This Together	The Fragile	Nothing
Drum Trip	When I Woke	Mercury
	Baroque Treasures, Vol. 2	Laserlight
Für Elise	Beethoven at Bedtime	Philips
	Violin Concerts, Romances	Deutsche Grammophon
Allegretto	Great Performances of the Twentieth Century	BBC Legends
Jupiter	The Planets	London
Help Me	Court and Spark	Elektra
Come Down from the Tree	How Glory Goes	Nonesuch
Persuance	Love Supreme	Impulse
Great Day	After Hours	Blue Note
In a Stone Circle	Divinities	EMI Angel
Venus	The Planets	Decca
	Piano Works	EMI
Puisque je suis fumeux	Ars Magis Subtiliter	New Albion
As Falls Wichita	As Falls Wichita	ECM
	World of Gregorian Chant	Pro Arte
Music for Airports	Ambient	Cala Recordings
Eternal Morning	Atmospheres and Nature's Retreats	St. Clair

Notes

Introduction:

1. Sufi Inayat Khan, *Music* (New York: Samuel Weiser, Inc., 1962), 8.

Chapter 1: *Your Essential Musical Intelligence*

1. Kirk Franklin, *God's Property* (B–Rite Music, 1997).
2. *The I Ching or Book of Changes* (Princeton: Princeton University Press, 1950), 68.
3. Robert Bly, *The Kabir Book* (Boston: Beacon Press, 1993).
4. Doc Childre and Howard Martin, *The HeartMath Solution* (San Francisco: HarperSanFrancisco, 1999), 31.

Chapter 2: *Music of the Body*

1. Kahil Gibran, *The Prophet* (New York: Knopf, 1951).
2. Swami Rama, Rudolph Ballentine, and Swami Ajaya, *Yoga and Psychotherapy: The Evolution of Consciousness* (Honesdale, PA: Himalayan Institute, 1976), 98.
3. Steven Locke and Douglas Colligan, *The Healer Within* (New York: Mentor Books, 1986), 19.
4. Randall McClellan, *The Healing Forces of Music* (Element, Inc., 1991), 38.
5. "Physiology, Mathematics, Music, and Medicine: Definitions and Concepts for Research," in *MusicMedicine,* ed. Rosalie Rebollo Pratt and Ralph Spintge (St. Louis: MMB Music, Inc.), 3.
6. Louise Montello, Ted Coons, and Jay Kantor, "The Use of

Group Music Therapy as a Treatment for Musical Performance Stress," *Medical Problems of Performing Artists* 5, no. 1 (1990): 49–57.

7. Edgar E. Coons, Louise Montello, et al., "Confidence and Denial Factors Affect Musicians' Postperformance Immune Response," *International Journal of Arts Medicine* 4, no. 1 (1995): 4–14.
8. Phil Nuernberger, *Freedom from Stress* (Honesdale, PA: Himalayan Institute, 1991), 51.
9. Dale Bartlett, et al., "The Effects of Music Listening and Perceived Sensory Experiences on the Immune System as Measured by Interleukin-1 and Cortisol," *Journal of Music Therapy* 30 (1993): 194–209.
10. Barry B. Bittman, et al., "Composite Effects of Group Drumming Music Therapy on Modulation of Neuroendocrine-Immune Parameters in Normal Subjects," *Alternative Therapies* 7, no. 1 (January 2002): 38.
11. George Leonard, *The Silent Pulse* (New York: Bantam, 1978), xii.
12. Hans Jenny, *Cymatics*, vol. 2 (Basilius Press, 1974), 7.
13. Ian Wickramasekera, "Secrets Kept from the Mind but Not the Body or Behavior: The Unsolved Problems of Identifying and Treating Somatization and Psychophysiological Disease," *Advances* 14, no. 2 (Spring 1998): 79–164.
14. Ernest Rossi, *The Psychobiology of Mind-Body Healing* (New York: W. W. Norton & Co., 1986), 41.
15. Laurel Keyes, *Toning: The Creative Power of the Voice* (Marina del Rey, CA: DeVorss, 1978).
16. Pir Vilayat Khan, *Alchemical Retreat* at the Abode of the Message, New Lebanon, New York, 1985.
17. Don Michel and Chris Chesky, "Music and Music Vibration for Pain Relief," ed. R. R. Pratt and R. Spintge, *MusicMedicine*, vol. 2 (Saint Louis: MMB Music, Inc., 1996), 218–226.

18. At the Addiction Research Center, "Music/Endorphin Link," *Brain/Mind Bulletin* (January 21 and February 11, 1985): 1–3.

CHAPTER 3: *Music as Life Force Energy*

1. Hazrat Inayat Kahn, *The Music of Life* (New Lebanon: Omega Press, 1983), 201.
2. John Diamond, M.D., workshop on *Life Energy in Music*, March 1987.
3. Tim Wilson, *Chant: The Healing Power of Voice and Ear* (Dallas: Sound of Light, 1984), audiocassette.
4. Paramahansa Yogananda, *Autobiography of a Yogi* (Los Angeles: Self-Realization Fellowship, 1946).
5. Swami Rama, Rudolph Ballentine, M.D., and Alan Hymes, M.D., *Science of Breath* (Honesdale, PA: Himalayan International Institute, 1979).
6. Harish Johari, *Breath, Mind, and Consciousness* (Rochester, VT: Destiny Books, 1989).
7. Yogeshwarananda Saraswati, *Science of Soul* (Yoga Niketan Trust, 1964).
8. Charanjit Ghooi, *Bhakti and Health* (Delhi: B. R. Publishing Corporation, 1996).
9. Swami Ajaya, *Psychotherapy East and West: A Unifying Paradigm* (Honesdale, PA: Himalayan Institute, 1983).
10. John Beaulieu, *Music and Sound in the Healing Arts* (Barrytown: Station Hill Press, 1987).

CHAPTER 4: *Music as Mind: Witnessing*

1. C. G. Jung, *Analytical Psychology, Its Theory and Practice* (New York: Pantheon, 1968).

2. Christopher Bollas, *The Shadow of the Object* (New York: Columbia University Press, 1987).
3. Diagram of the Vedanta Conception of Mind from *Yoga and Psychotherapy* (Honesdale, PA: Himalayan Press, 1976), 71.
4. Daniel Goleman, *Emotional Intelligence* (New York: Bantam Books, 1995).
5. R. E. Dafter, "Why 'negative' emotions can sometimes be positive; the spectrum model of emotions and their role in mind-body healing," *Advances: The Journal of Mind-Body Health* 12 (1999): 6–19.
6. James W. Pennebaker, *Opening Up* (New York: Guilford Press, 1997).
7. Dale Barlett, Donald Kaufman and Roger Smeltekop, "The Effects of Music Listening and Perceived Sensory Experiences on the Immune System as Measured by Interleukin-I and Cortisol," *Journal of Music Therapy* 30, no. 4 (1993).
8. Deforia Lane, "The Effect of a Single Music Therapy Session on Hospitalized Children as Measured by Salivary Immunoglobulin A, Speech Pause Time, and a Patient Opinion Likert Scale," *Pediatric Research* 29, no. 4, part I (1991).
9. Pinchas Noy, "The Psychodynamic Meaning of Music," *Journal of Music Therapy* (March 1967): 8.
10. Rolando Benenzon, M.D., *Music Therapy in Child Psychosis* (St. Louis: MMB Music, 1982).
11. Motherese—PBS Special, "The Birth of Language," September, 1993.
12. Daniel N. Stern, *Diary of a Baby* (New York: Basic Books, 1990).
13. Daniel N. Stern, *The Interpersonal World of the Infant* (New York: BasicBooks, 1985), 53–61.
14. Suzanne Langer, *Philosophy in a New Key* (Cambridge: Harvard University Press, 1942).

15. Avram Goldstein, "Thrills in Response to Music and Other Stimuli," *Physiological Psychology* 8 (1989): 126–129.
16. Donald W. Winnicott, *Playing and Reality* (Tavistock: London, 1971).

CHAPTER 5: *Music as Mind: Playing*

1. Howard Gardner, *Frames of Mind* (New York: Basic Books, 1985).
2. Louise Montello, "The Perils of Perfectionism," *Allegro* (September 1999): 13–15.
3. Jean Berger, "Heart" from *Four Songs* (based on poems by Langston Hughes from *Fields of Wonder* (New York: Alfred A. Knopf, Inc., 1938, 1947).
4. Arthur Schopenhauer, *The World as Will and Representation*, vols. I and II, trans. E. F. J. Payne (New York: Dover, 1966).
5. Pir Vilayat Inayat Khan, *Introducing Spirituality into Counseling and Therapy* (Lebanon Springs: Omega Press, 1982), 156.

CHAPTER 6: *Music as Intellect/Intuition*

1. Swami Ajaya, *Psychotherapy East and West*, (Honesdale, PA: Himalayan International Institute, 1983), 243.
2. Ibid., 248.
3. Roberto Assagioli, M.D., *Act of Will* (Baltimore: Penguin Books, 1974).
4. Swami Rama, Rudolph Ballentine, and Alan Hymes, *Science of Breath* (Honesdale, PA: Himalayan International Institute, 1979), 104.
5. Hazrat Inayat Khan, *The Music of Life* (New Lebanon: Omega Press, 1988).
6. Kenneth Sylvan Guthrie, *The Pythagorean Sourcebook and Library*

(Grand Rapids, MI: Phanes Press, 1987), 95.

7. Alice Miller, *The Drama of the Gifted Child* (New York: Basic Books, 1981).
8. Marshall McLuhan, *The Medium is the Message* (New York: Bantam Books, 1967).
9. Larry Dossey, M.D., *Meaning and Medicine* (New York: Bantam Books, 1991).
10. Helen L. Bonny and Louis M. Savary, *Music and Your Mind* (New York: Station Hill Press, 1990).
11. Susanne F. Fincher, *Creating Mandalas* (Boston: Shambhala, 1991).

Chapter 7: *Music of Bliss*

1. William Wordsworth, *The Prelude; or Growth of a Poet's Mind*, edited from the ms., with introduction, text, and critical notes by Ernest De Selincourt (Oxford: Clarendon Press, 1959).
2. Ken Wilber, Jack Engler, and Daniel P. Brown, *Transformations of Consciousness* (Boston: Shambhala, 1986).
3. Shirley Rabb Winston, *Music as the Bridge* (Virginia Beach, VA: A.R.E. Press, 1972).
4. Robert Gass, *Chanting* (New York: Broadway Books, 1999).
5. Kate Marks, *Circle of Songs* (Lenox, MA: Full Circle Press, 1993).
6. Thanks to David Hykes for training in overtone chanting.
7. Alfred A. Tomatis, M.D. "The Spirituality of the Voice," *Material for Thought* 11 (San Francisco: Far West Editions, Autumn 1986).
8. Ramon Llull, *Abre de filosofia d'amor/Ramon Llull* (Barcelona: Barcino, 1980).
9. *The Impersonal Life* (Marina del Rey, CA: DeVorss & Co., 1941).

10. James G. Vargiu, "The Theory: Subpersonalities," *Synthesis* I, no. I (1974): 9–47.

CHAPTER 8: *Music of Trauma*

1. Judith L. Herman, *Trauma and Recovery* (New York: Basic Books, 1992).
2. Louise Montello, "A Psychoanalytic Music Therapy Approach to Treating Traumatized Adults," *Music Therapy Perspectives* 17, no. 2 (1999): 75.
3. Donald W. Winnicott, "Transitional Objects and Transitional Phenomena," *Collected Papers* (New York: Basic Books, 1958).
4. Montello, 76.
5. Louise Montello, "Relational Issues in Psychoanalytic Music Therapy with Traumatized Individuals," in *The Dynamics of Music Psychotherapy*, ed. Kenneth Bruscia (New Hampshire: Barcelona Publishers, 1998), 301.
6. Pir Vilayat Khan, from *Alchemical Retreat* at Abode of the Message, October 1988.
7. John Bradshaw, *Homecoming: Reclaiming and Championing Your Inner Child* (New York: Bantam, 1992); interesting ideas on child development; also *Bradshaw on: The Family* (Health Communications, Inc., 1988).
8. Pandit Rajmani Tigunait, *The Power of Mantra and the Mystery of Initiation* (Honesdale, PA: Yoga International Books, 1996).
9. Swami Rama, *The Path of Fire and Light*, vol. II (Honesdale, PA: Himalayan International Institute, 1988).
10. Hazrat Inayat Khan, *The Sufi Message of Hazrat Inayat Khan*, vol. 5 (Geneva: International Headquarters Sufi Movement, 1979), 137.

Notes

Notes

Suggested Readings

Davies, J. M., and M. G. Frawley. *Treating the Adult Survivor of Childhood Sexual Abuse.* New York: Basic Books, 1994.

Gardner, Kay. *Sounding the Inner Landscape.* San Francisco: Harper Collins, 1997.

Lingerman, Hal A. *The Healing Energies of Music.* Wheaton, IL: Quest Books, 1995.

Lingerman, Hal A. *Life Streams: Journeys into Meditation and Music.* Wheaton, IL: Quest Books, 1988.

Maslow, Abraham H. *The Farther Reaches of Human Nature.* New York: Penguin Books, 1971.

Montello, Louise. "Exploring the Causes and Treatment of Musical Performance Stress: A Process Oriented Group Music Therapy Approach." In *Music Medicine,* edited by R. Spintge and R. Droh. St. Louis: MMB Music, Inc., 1992.

Psychological Trauma. Edited by Bessel van der Kolk. Washington, DC: American Psychiatric Press, 1987.

Rudhyar, Dane. *The Magic of Tone and the Art of Music.* Boulder: Shambhala, 1982.

Schopenhauer, Arthur. *The World as Will and Representation.* Vol. 1, trans. E. F. J. Payne. New York: Dover, 1966.

Swami Rama, Rudolph Ballentine, and Alan Hymes. *The Science of Breath.* Honesdale, PA: Himalayan Institute, 1979.

Terr, Lenore C. "Childhood Traumas: An Outline and Overview." *American Journal of Psychiatry* 148 (1991): 1020.

Tomatis, Alfred A. *The Conscious Ear.* New York: Station Hill Press, 1991.

The Upanishads. Translated by Juan Mascaro. New York: Penguin Books, 1965.

Glossary

alchemy – mystical process of turning dark (lead) into light (gold)

altered state – states that are qualitatively different from normal waking consciousness

apana – breath current associated with downward energy flow (on exhalation)

archetypes – primordial images, similar to cultural motifs, represented everywhere throughout history; their main features are their power, depth, and autonomy; innate, inherited patterns of psychological performance, linked to instinct and, when activated, manifested in behavior and emotion

autonomic nervous system – the portion of the nervous system concerned with regulation of the cardiac muscle, heartbeat, digestion, smooth muscle tissue, and the glandular system

Ayurvedic five-element system – earth, water, fire, air, ether, components that make up all of life as we know it

beingness – the wave of serenity that instantly connects us to our essential nature, which is bliss, consciousness, and beauty

cellular memory – body-based, as opposed to cognitive or ego-based memory; infants process memories in this way, as do people who have been traumatized

chakra – means literally, "wheel" or "circle"; in Eastern philosophic tradition, one of seven or more centers of consciousness located along the spine from the coccyx to the top of the head

chanting – singing praise to the Divinity that exists both within and without

collective unconscious – innate psychological activity that transcends personal experience and relates directly to the archetypal and instinctual bases of human life (i.e. witch, hero)

consciousness – state of being; awareness

core self – the infinitely healthy, creative, forward-moving essence of being

cortisol – stress hormone

defense mechanism – the ego's active struggle to protect against danger—typically disapproval, loss of love, and loss of power—and their attendant unpleasant affects during development and throughout life

diaphragm – dome-shaped muscle that attaches to lowest two ribs and separates thoracic cavity from abdominal cavity; pushes down when we inhale; rises up to push stale air out when we exhale

dissociation – a split between mind and body as a defense against somatic dysfunction and psychic conflict

dissonance – discord, lack of harmony

ego – aspect of consciousness that organizes sense impressions from the perspective of the personal "I"

emotions – innate psychobiological signals that serve as sources of information for the psychologically aware individual, emanating from the four primary instinctual urges: self-preservation, sleep, food, and sex

endorphins – substance produced by and released from the brain that acts as a powerful pain killer and mood enhancer

entrainment – tendency of individuals and objects to synchronize to a dominant rhythm

Essential Musical Intelligence – natural ability to use music and sound as self-reflecting, transformational tools to facilitate total health and well-being

false self – a defensive character structure that protects the real, vulnerable, creative self from injury and/or betrayal by self-absorbed and/or abusive caretakers; "as-if" personality

fight-or-flight reaction – sympathetic nervous system reaction that prepares the body to fight or flee in response to a threat

grace – revelation or gift from the higher self

great chain of being – the yogic concept of sheaths; includes body, energy/breath, mind, intellect/intuition, and bliss

higher power – the omnipotent, omniscient aspect of self at the core of all beings

higher self – part of us that is connected with Divine Essence; core self

holding environment – nonspecific, supportive continuity provided by the felt presence of the good-enough mother

holding tension – ability to sit with difficult feelings

homeostasis – the normal state of the body in which it is able to maintain a uniform state of health

hypervigilance – extreme watchfulness; inability to relax

hypnogogic state – intermediary state between waking and dreaming characterized by theta brain waves

ida – one of three major energy channels, corresponding to lunar energy and situated on the left side of the spinal column

impersonal stance – state of complete equanimity and receptivity to divine inspiration and guidance

inner music – mostly inaudible backdrop of consciousness (emotional/instinctual) that accompanies us as we develop through the various stages of life

introjects – internalized characteristics of primary caretakers that can take on a life of their own when not consciously realized

iso principle – a music therapy concept whereby the therapist, when selecting music within the therapeutic context, first tries to match the mood of the client before attempting to move the client into a more desirable feeling state (*iso* means "same")

kokoro – mind of the heart (Japanese)

left-brain hemisphere – analytical and sequential functioning; verbal skills

maladaptive – unhelpful, negative, or destructive

limbic system – brain center associated with emotions and instincts

mandala – circular drawings that act as containers for symbolic material from the inner life

mantra – universal seed syllable(s) of divinity used as object of meditation

mantra meditation – the practice of sitting quietly and repeating a mantra over and over with complete concentration until the mind merges with the essence of the mantra and achieves a state of deep peace and equilibrium

mystic – an individual who seeks to transcend the constraints of the ego through direct, subjective experience of the Divine

Motherese – the unique pattern of sounds that caregivers the world over use to communicate with infants; melodic speech communicated at significantly higher pitch levels

musical self-statement – an improvisational snapshot of the inner life at a particular point in time

nada yoga – sacred science of sound

nigguns – traditional Jewish songs without words

om (aum) – universal mantra; stands for the waking, dreaming, and sleeping states; the silent part represents the fourth state, *turiya* (bliss)

overtones – series of barely audible higher-pitched tones that originate from a single fundamental tone and that give color and uniqueness to musical instruments and the human voice

paradox – technique of ancient wisdom traditions that uses contradiction to break through the duality of opposites to a deeper truth of union and oneness

parasympathetic nervous system – one of two subdivisions of the autonomic nervous system (the other is the sympathetic nervous system); slows the body down and aids in digestion, elimination, and relaxation

peak experience – moment of bliss in which we are in touch with the perfection of our true nature

personal unconscious – forgotten and/or repressed memories

pingala – one of three major energy channels situated along the right side of the spinal column, corresponding to the body's solar energy

polarity – an extreme in which one aspect of a pair of opposites is experienced as desirable while the other is judged as inferior and/or repulsive

proactive – responsible for self

psychoneuroimmunology – branch of medicine that studies interrelationships between mind (psycho), nervous system (neuro) and immune system (immunology)

right-brain hemisphere – emotional, receptive, integrative, being aspect of consciousness; musical

samana – breath current associated with solar plexus; fiery energy used to digest food, exert force, or dominate

self-reflecting – that which mirrors our inner lives

sensory-motor mind – receives sense impressions and coordinates them with motor responses

Shakti – Hindu goddess symbolizing one of the two original polaric forces (Shiva's female counterpart); giver of life; mistress of divine creation and the realm of form

sheaths – from yoga tradition, described as five levels of consciousness or being, with the more evolved level conceptualized as existing within another

Shiva – Hindu god symbolizing one of the two original polaric forces (Shakti's male counterpart); pure unmanifest consciousness;

consciousness without form

shushumna – highly creative state occurring briefly during the shift between right- and left-nostril dominance; can foster spontaneous healing and channeling of deeper sources of aesthetic beauty and wisdom

so-ham – "I am that"; universal mantra reflecting the natural sound of the breath (intone "so" on the inhalation, "ham" on the exhalation)

spectrum model of emotions – asserts that all emotions are innately neutral (neither good nor bad) and that mind-body healing utilizes the full spectrum of emotions

splitting – defensive mechanism whereby the fragile ego, unable to hold the tension between two conflicting feeling states about the same person, object, or event (e.g. love and hate toward performing), denies and renders frozen the more dangerous or inappropriate feeling state; the forbidden feeling is then split off (hidden from consciousness) in order to stave off confusion and anxiety

subpersonality – resistant part(s) of the self representing internalized aspects of one or both parents or other caregivers; split-off, developmentally arrested aspect of self (e.g. inner child)

symbol – accumulators, transformers, and conductors of psychological energies

sympathetic nervous system – part of the autonomic nervous system that tends to increase blood pressure and heartbeat and inhibit glandular secretions; prepares body for fight or flight

synesthesia – crossing of the senses whereby one sense is stimulated but the response occurs in another sense, i.e."hearing" colors, "seeing" sounds, "tasting" shapes, and so on; not to be confused with metaphor, as in poetry; accompanied by a sense of certitude or even a "eureka" feeling; not just a state of perception, but of knowledge

tantra – sacred dance of interpenetrating dualities; the yoga of reuniting duality, of restoring that which is separate into oneness

throat chakra – center of infinite space, higher creativity, inspiration, and nurturance; abode of the divine child

toning – intentional sound making for health and healing

trading fours – jazz technique whereby musicians in a combo take turns improvising four measures each on the form of a tune, playing off each other or creating original motifs

trance – altered state of consciousness

transitional object – the infant's first "not-me" possession, something inanimate but treasured that the child uses in the course of emotional separation from the primary love object, particularly during times of stress

transitional space – a field of play in which emotional dynamics emerging within the child's relationships with people and objects can be examined, experienced in symbol, thought about, and processed

udana – breath current that moves up and out; energetic force that powers the physiological act of vomiting

unitary consciousness – state in which all duality has been transcended; highest goal on the yoga path

unstruck sound – center of bliss in the cave of the heart

unthought known – body-based (cellular) memory of the emotional climate of life; world during the first few years of life internalized as "inner music," which is experienced as an almost imperceptible, yet pervasive mood (e.g. hunger, melancholy, anxiety) that is indelibly woven into the fabric of consciousness

vitality affects – properties of feelings (as well as of music) that represent the underlying, nonreferential dynamic elements associated with specific emotional states

vyana – breath current associated with circulation of energy throughout whole body; development of body image and sexuality

witnessing – process of turning focus inward and becoming an impartial observer of the permutations of body, mind, and emotions

witnessing stance – position of self-observation and inner listening

yantra – geometric diagram, often composed of a small dot surrounded by circles, triangles, and squares (each of which is symbolic), used as a meditative focus

Index

A

B

O

P

R

S

T

U

V

W

Y

Z

Credits

Grateful acknowledgment is made for permission to reprint copyrighted material:

Images on pp. 41 and 42 from *Cymatics: A Study of Wave Phenomena and Vibration,* by Hans Jenny. © 2001 MACROmedia. Used by permission of MACROmedia, 219 Grant Road, Newmarket, NH 03857. www.cymaticsource.com

From *The Ķabir Book* by Robert Bly. Copyright © 1971, 1977 by Robert Bly. © 1977 by the Seventies Press. Reprinted by permission of Beacon Press, Boston.

From *Diary of a Baby,* by Daniel N. Stern. New York, Basic Books, 1990. Used by permission of Perseus Books.

From *The Collected Poems of Langston Hughes* by Langston Hughes, copyright © 1994 by The Estate of Langston Hughes. Used by permission of Alfred A. Knopf, a division of Random House, Inc.

Diagrams on pp. 72, 89, and illustration on p. 137 from *Yoga and Psychotherapy: The Evolution of Consciousness* by Swami Rama, Rudolph Ballantine, and Swami Ajaya. Honesdale, Pa., The Himalayan Institute, © 1976. Used by permission of the Himalayan Institute.

Chart on p. 135 from *Psychotherapy East and West: A Unifying Paradigm* by Swami Ajaya. Honesdale, Pa., The Himalayan Institute, © 1983. Used by permission of the Himalayan Institute.

From *The Sufi Message of Hazrat Inayat Khan,* vol. 5. Geneva, International Headquarters Sufi Movement, 1979. Reprinted by permission of The Sufi Movement, The Netherlands.

Every effort has been made to secure permission for material quoted in this book. Any additional copyright holders are invited to contact the publisher so that proper credit can be given in future editions.

QUEST BOOKS
are published by
The Theosophical Society in America,
Wheaton, Illinois 60189-0270,
a branch of a world fellowship,
a membership organization
dedicated to the promotion of the unity of
humanity and the encouragement of the study of
religion, philosophy, and science, to the end that
we may better understand ourselves and our place in
the universe. The Society stands for complete
freedom of individual search and belief.
For further information about its activities,
write, call 1-800-669-1571, e-mail olcott@theosmail.net
or consult its Web page: http://www.theosophical.org

The Theosophical Publishing House
is aided by the generous support of
THE KERN FOUNDATION,
a trust established by Herbert A. Kern
and dedicated to Theosophical education.

Praise for Louise Montello's

Essential Musical Intelligence

Louise Montello's book brings a far ranging perspective and deep insight into the field of music and healing. This new and innovative material will open the door, for music lovers and health care professionals alike, to the majesty and power of healing with sound.

—*Glen Velez, percussionist, composer, and performer whose audio CDs include* Rhythms of the Chakras *and* Breathing Rhythms

Louise Montello points out wisely that each person *IS* music. She demonstrates how each of us is continuously vibrating and radiating our own energy field, composed of dimensions of body, emotions, mind, soul, will, and spirit. Experiencing and making beautiful music attunes us to the larger realms of Light and the many frequencies of energy and consciousness available to us and waiting to be awakened. For readers in our diversified world today, it is important to give specific examples of music that has proved to be therapeutic. The author suggests many particular musical selections that can help to balance the listener physiologically, emotionally, psychologically, and spiritually. These selections range across many genres of music and include classical, popular, New Age and world compositions. I especially enjoyed Dr. Montello's multicultural orientation, both musically and spiritually. She also lists personal case studies where music has helped individuals with different needs. I believe that her work is informative and inspirational, while yet respecting the mysterious and subjective ways in which different musical selections and performances affect each of us so uniquely. Read this book!

—*Hal A. Lingerman, M.A., M. Div., author of* The Healing Energies of Music

*M*usic is an essential bridge uniting mind, body, and spirit. Essential Musical Intelligence is your personal road map for healing.

—Barry Bittman, M.D., CEO of the Mind-Body Wellness Center in Meadville, Pennsylvania and author of Reprogramming Pain

*I*t is a testament to the truth of this book that the text alone transmits its healing vibrations, even without the music. Certainly the book inspires the sense of good will and hope, blessedness, wisdom, and faith that channel and nurture our energies for health. The symphony that is man reflects and resonates with the symphony that is creation, and between is the space wherein we, each one of us, strive to find and grasp the spiritual nature of who and how we are. Dr. Montello opens up this space, illuminates it, and advises us how to navigate the mysteries of everyday miracles and reach out to touch the immense treasure that awaits our claim. It is impossible to read her work without feeling its strength coursing through one's body and to joyfully feel better for it. Share it with countless others. This book will have a joyous destiny.

—Clive E. Robbins, D.H.L., D.M.M., M.T.-B.C., founder of the Nordoff-Robbins Music Therapy Center in London and New York City; music therapist and master teacher; coauthor of Creative Music Therapy

*I*n the hands of this master, an exquisite spirituality guides and deepens our experience of music. Montello brings to her writing the insights of a fine performer, a gifted teacher, and an experienced psychoanalyst. Her work in transforming lives is brought herein to a new dimension. You will be changed for the better if you read this book!

—Eli H. Newberger, M.D., pediatrician, musician, and author of The Men They Will Become: The Nature and Nurture of Male Character